Handbook To The Cathedrals Of England, Volume 1

Richard John King

YORK CATHEDRAL. WEST END.

HANDBOOK

TO THE

CATHEDRALS OF ENGLAND.

[5]

Northern Division.

PART I.

YORK.—RIPON.—CARLISLE.

With Illustrations.

LONDON:

JOHN MURRAY, ALBEMARLE STREET.

1869.

UNIFORM WITH THE PRESENT WORK.

———◆◇◆———

THE SOUTHERN CATHEDRALS OF ENGLAND: containing WINCHESTER, SALISBURY, EXETER, WELLS, CHICHESTER, ROCHESTER, CANTERBURY. With 200 Illustrations. 2 vols. Crown 8vo. 24s.

THE EASTERN CATHEDRALS OF ENGLAND: containing OXFORD, PETERBOROUGH, ELY, NORWICH, LINCOLN. With 95 Illustrations. Post 8vo. 18s.

THE WESTERN CATHEDRALS OF ENGLAND: containing BRISTOL, GLOUCESTER, WORCESTER, HEREFORD, LICHFIELD. With 50 Illustrations. Post 8vo. 16s.

LONDON: PRINTED BY W. CLOWES AND SONS, STAMFORD STREET,
AND CHARING CROSS.

PREFACE.

———◦◦———

THE two parts into which it has been found necessary to divide the HANDBOOK TO THE NORTHERN CATHEDRALS, contain, in the first, York, Ripon, and Carlisle; in the second, Durham, Chester, and Manchester.

Of these Cathedrals, York alone has been described by Professor Willis. His elaborate and most valuable history, which is contained in the York volume of the Archæological Institute, has been referred to and used throughout.

Acknowledgment of much kind interest and assistance is also due from me to the Rev. James Raine, Canon of York; to the Rev. William Greenwell, Minor Canon and Precentor of Durham; to the Very Rev. the Dean of Chester; to John Richard Walbran, Esq., of Fall Croft, Ripon; to the Rev. G. A. Poole, of Welford; and to Mr. James P. Holden, Architect of the Cathedral at Manchester.

RICHARD JOHN KING.

b

LIST OF ILLUSTRATIONS.

———•◦•———

NORTHERN CATHEDRALS.—PART I.

York.

PLAN.

TITLE-PAGE—Corbel in Transept.

FRONTISPIECE—the West Front.

		PAGE
I. South-east View . . . . *to face*	10
Showing the double plane of tracery of the Choir.	
II. Western Transept . . . . *to face*	12
From within the South entrance, showing the " Five Sisters of York."	
III. Corbel in South Transept (*see* Title-page).	
IV. Monument of Archbishop Gray . *to face*	17
V. Monument of Archbishop Greenfield . ,,	23
VI. Nave from the East . . . ,,	25
Inscription in Chapter House.	43
VII. Interior of Chapter House . . *to face*	44
VIII. Choir from the West . . . ,,	47
IX. Horn of Ulphus, and Details . . ,,	83
X. Exterior of Chapter House . . ,,	89
XI. East End . . . . . ,,	91
The iron railing is omitted in this View.	

Ripon.

PLAN.

TITLE-PAGE—Corbel in South Aisle of Choir.

PAGE

FRONTISPIECE—West Front.

In this View some of the houses at the end of Kirkgate are omitted, in order to show the front more perfectly.

I. Windows in the West Front . . *to face* 151

As they were before the restoration, at which time the tracery was removed.

II. Nave from the East . . . . *to face* 154

Sculpture on Monument in Nave . . . 156

III. Choir from the West . . . *to face* 162

IV. North Aisle of Choir . . . „ 165

Plan of St. Wilfrid's Crypt 170

V. St. Wilfrid's Crypt . . . . *to face* 170

The first figure shows the passage at the back, with the opening through the Needle (a) into the larger cell.

VI. North Door . . . . . „ 174

VII. Capitals of North Door . . . „ 174

VIII. Early Norman Crypt, Chapter House and Lady Loft . . . . . . „ 175

IX. South-east View . . . . . „ 176

Carlisle.

PLAN.

TITLE-PAGE — Monumental Recesses in North Aisle of Choir.

FRONTISPIECE—East End.

I. Well in South Transept, and Screen of St. Catherine's Chapel . . . *to face* 197

II. Choir . . . . . . „ 199

III. Monumental Recesses (*see* Title-page).

IV. South View . . . . . „ 211

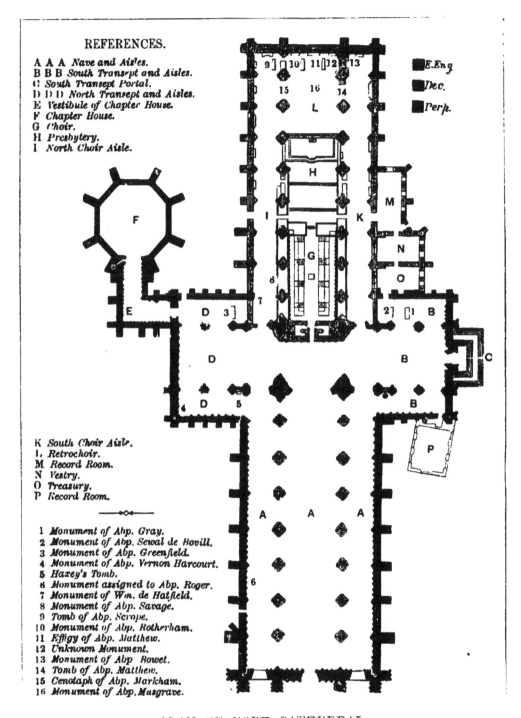

REFERENCES.

A A A *Nave and Aisles.*
B B B *South Transept and Aisles.*
C *South Transept Portal.*
D D D *North Transept and Aisles.*
E *Vestibule of Chapter House.*
F *Chapter House.*
G *Choir.*
H *Presbytery.*
I *North Choir Aisle.*

K *South Choir Aisle.*
L *Retrochoir.*
M *Record Room.*
N *Vestry.*
O *Treasury.*
P *Record Room.*

1 *Monument of Abp. Gray.*
2 *Monument of Abp. Sewal de Bovill.*
3 *Monument of Abp. Greenfield.*
4 *Monument of Abp. Vernon Harcourt.*
5 *Haxey's Tomb.*
6 *Monument assigned to Abp. Roger.*
7 *Monument of Wm. de Hatfield.*
8 *Monument of Abp. Savage.*
9 *Tomb of Abp. Scrope.*
10 *Monument of Abp. Rotherham.*
11 *Effigy of Abp. Matthew.*
12 *Unknown Monument.*
13 *Monument of Abp Bowet.*
14 *Tomb of Abp. Matthew.*
15 *Cenotaph of Abp. Markham.*
16 *Monument of Abp. Musgrave.*

E.Eng
Dec.
Perp.

PLAN OF YORK CATHEDRAL.

Scale of 100 feet to 1 inch.

YORK CATHEDRAL.

CORBEL IN SOUTH TRANSEPT.

YORK CATHEDRAL.

PART I.

History and Details.

I. THE chief authorities for the architectural history of the existing cathedral at York are the "Chronica Pontificum Ecclesiæ Eboraci," by the Dominican Thomas Stubbes, ranging from the foundation of the see to the death of Archbishop Thoresby in 1373; and the series of Fabric Rolls and other documents in the custody of the Dean and Chapter.[*]

Before describing the Minster as it exists at present, it will be necessary to give some account of the churches which have preceded it on the same site.

[*] The chronicle of Stubbes will be found in Twysden's Decem Scriptores. The 'Fabric Rolls' have been edited by Canon Raine for the Surtees Society. The 'Architectural History' of the cathedral, by Professor Willis, will be found in the York volume of the Archæological Institute, and is, of course, most valuable and important. Very great use has necessarily been made of it in the following account. Two other modern histories must also be mentioned here, the 'Historical and Descriptive Guide,' by Messrs. Poole and Hugall; and the 'History of the Metropolitan Church of St. Peter, at York,' by John Browne. Frequent reference has been made to both.

Although the Roman Eboracum can hardly have been without a Christian church, all recollection of such a building seems to have passed away when St. Paulinus visited Northumbria at the beginning of the seventh century. The king, Eadwin, who then embraced Christianity, was baptised (Easter-day, A.D. 627) in a small wooden church, hastily built whilst he was receiving instruction as a catechumen, and dedicated to St. Peter. This was the first church built on the site of the existing Minster. After his baptism, in the words of Bede, the king "set about to construct in the same place, at the suggestion of Paulinus, a larger and more noble basilica of stone, in the midst of which the oratory which he had first built was to be included. Accordingly, having laid his foundations, he began to build his basilica in a square form around the original oratory; but, before the walls were completed, the king was slain, and it was left to his successor Oswald to complete the work."[b] The head of Eadwin, after his death in the battle of Heathfield (A.D. 633), was brought to York and deposited in this basilica, in the "porticus of St. Gregory the Pope, from whose disciples he had received the word of life."[c] Archbishop Wilfrid, in 669, found this building in great decay. He repaired its roofs and its walls, "rendering them whiter than snow,"[d] and filled the windows with glass. In the year 741, the "monas-

[b] Beda, H. E., L. ii. c. 14.
[c] Id. id., L. ii. c. 20.
[d] Parietes quoque lavans, super nivem dealbavit. Eddius, 59.

terium" or "minster" in York was burnt, according to Roger Hoveden; and Archbishop Albert, who came to the see in 767, is recorded by Alcuin as having been the builder of a most magnificent basilica in his metropolitan city. It has been doubted whether the verses of Alcuin record the rebuilding of the church founded by King Eadwin, or whether Archbishop Albert's new basilica was on a fresh site in a different part of the city. But it is scarcely possible to believe that York could at that time have contained two churches of such size and importance, and we may fairly conclude that Albert rebuilt the church founded by Eadwin and restored by Wilfrid. This church remained until the year 1069, when it was destroyed, in its turn, by fire, in the course of the Conqueror's devastation of Yorkshire. The central wall of the crypt below the choir of the existing Minster, is the only relic which can possibly be assigned to the Saxon cathedral of York.

THOMAS OF BAYEUX, the first Norman archbishop, was consecrated to the see in the year 1070. He found his cathedral in ruins, and is said first to have repaired it as well as he could, and afterwards (before the end of his episcopate in 1100) to have built a new church from the foundations. This church remained entire until Archbishop ROGER (1154—1181) pulled down the choir with its crypts, and reconstructed them on a considerably larger scale. Archbishop GRAY (1215—1255), in all probability, pulled down the south transept of Thomas of Bayeux's church, and built that which now exists. JOHN LE ROMEYN, or ROMANUS, sub-dean and treasurer of York (1228—1256) and Archdeacon of Richmond, built, according to Stubbes, the north transept and a central bell-tower at his own expense. The early Norman nave of Archbishop Thomas still remained; but its removal was begun in 1291, when Archbishop LE ROMEYN (1285—1296) son of the treasurer, laid the first stone of the existing nave, which was completed, after some intermissions, about the year 1345; although its wooden ceiling was not added until 1355. The chapter-house was in progress at the same time as the nave. Archbishop Roger's Norman choir was standing at the completion of the nave, but it was plainly out of character with the increased size and magnificence of the new building, and in 1361 Archbishop THORESBY (1352—1373) began the existing Lady Chapel and Presbytery, which were, no doubt, completed at the time of his death. Between the years 1373 and 1400 the Norman choir was entirely taken down, and was replaced by that which now exists. The central bell-tower, which had been the work of the treasurer John le Romeyn, was recased about 1405, and the works of the present tower extended over the succeeding years. The south-western tower was begun about 1432, whilst John Berningham was treasurer; the north-western was completed about 1470; and on the 3rd of July, 1472, the church, which had thus been completely rebuilt, was reconsecrated, and the day was afterwards observed as the feast of dedication. Like the first wooden church of Paulinus, the vast Minster was dedicated in the name of God and of St. Peter the Apostle.

The Minster (in spite of the name " minster," or " monasterium," frequently applied to it by early writers) was never occupied by monks; but from a very early time by a body of secular canons, who retained the name of "Culdees" until the reign of Henry I. The name Culdee (Gille De, Child of God) was that given to the first Scottish religious who established themselves at Iona under St. Columba; and in York it was no doubt a relic of the teaching of Aidan, who, after the expulsion of St. Paulinus, was sent from Iona as a missionary into Northumbria.

The dates and architectural character of the different portions of the cathedral may be thus recapitulated :—

Saxon, of uncertain date.—Inner wall of crypt.

Norman (*temp.* Archbishop Thomas, 1070—1100). —Remains at western end of crypt.

Late Norman (*temp.* Archbishop Roger, 1154—1181). —Eastern portion of crypt.

Early English (1215—1256). — North and south transepts.

Decorated (1285—1345).—Nave and chapter-house.

Early Perpendicular (1361—1373).—Lady chapel and presbytery.

Perpendicular (1373—1400).—Choir.

Late Perpendicular (1405—1470).—Central and two western towers.

The Minster is built of magnesian limestone, from

quarries near Tadcaster; from the Huddlestone quarries, near Sherburn; and from quarries near Stapleton (Pontefract). A body of workmen (not so large as that which the Fabric Rolls show to have been anciently in the constant service of the chapter) is kept for the execution of repairs, on which considerable sums are spent yearly.

II. York Minster has, perhaps, a more widely-extended reputation than any other English cathedral. Until the rise of the great manufacturing towns within the present century, York, like the Roman Eboracum which it replaced, was by far the most important city in the north of England. It was the centre from which Christianity had been dispersed throughout the country north of the Humber, and the church in which Paulinus baptised King Eadwin was, as we have seen, long preserved within the walls of the existing cathedral. The wealth and importance of the ancient city, and the memory of the great change of faith in Northumbria, found their most permanent representation in the Minster, which, as the metropolitan church of the northern province, gathered about it the recollections, often of deep historical interest, connected with its long series of archbishops. These causes sufficiently explain the early fame of the cathedral, and after the completion of the long series of works which have just been recorded, the size and grandeur of the building itself rapidly extended its reputation. Æneas Sylvius, afterwards Pope Pius II., who passed through York about the year 1430, soon after the central tower had

been finished, describes the church as "worthy to be
noted throughout the world (*toto orbe memorandum*)
for its size and architecture; with a very light chapel
(*sacellum lucidissimum*, the chapter-house? or the retrochoir?), whose glass walls" (the large windows) rise
"between very slender clustered columns." The shrine
of St. William, the great treasure of the Minster,
although, no doubt, rich and stately, was exceeded in
importance by that of St. Cuthbert at Durham, and
probably by those of St. John at Beverley, and St.
Wilfrid at Ripon; but the cathedral itself was always
the great centre of the northern counties, and it still
remains a bond of union between the many sects, parties,
and classes scattered over the three Ridings. Whatever
touches the Minster touches the heart of Yorkshire.

Although other English cathedrals can show portions and details of better design and of more delicate
beauty, it must be admitted that few exceed York
Minster in dignity and massive grandeur. These are
especially the characteristics of the exterior. It is
not easy to find a point near at hand from which a
good general view is commanded; but from the walk
on the walls the cathedral is well seen, towering above
the ancient city, and reflecting on its stately towers
and roofs every change in the sky that bends over the
great plain of York. Of the nearer views the best
are—that of the west front, from the end of the space
before it, which, within the last few years, has been
cleared of many cottages and decaying buildings; and
that of the whole north side, from the lawn in front of

the Deanery. In the height of its roofs (99½ feet in the nave, 102 feet in the choir) York exceeds every other English cathedral. This great height is evident on the exterior, where, to some extent, it dwarfs the apparent dimensions of the central and western towers, and it is the main cause of the first powerful impression on entering the building. The great breadth of the nave (104¼ feet, with its aisles) is ill-supported by the comparatively slender piers of the main arcade, which want the grandeur of the Norman piers at Ely or Peterborough, or of the more massive Perpendicular arcades in the naves of Winchester and Canterbury. The breadth of the choir (99½ feet) is somewhat less, but it combines with the square eastern end filled with one of the largest windows in the world—a literal " wall of glass "—and with the lines of the aisle-walls —unbroken by chantries or side-chapels—to produce an effect which differs altogether from that of the more picturesque choirs of Lincoln, Salisbury, or Wells. In them the varied and interesting lines and the different elevations of chantries and eastern transepts—and in the two latter a peculiar arrangement of piers in the retrochoir — cause an intricacy which is especially pleasant to the eye and the imagination. In York the whole is seen at once ; but the first impression is that of extreme grandeur and dignity, and it may safely be said that, in proportion as the cathedral becomes better known, and the eye becomes more capable of measuring its vast spaces, this impression—so far, at least, as the choir is concerned—is steadily increased. The view across the great transept takes its place, without question, among the finest architectural views in Europe.

The transept aisles are vaulted with stone. The original roofs of both nave and choir were of wood, probably on account of the unusual breadth of the space to be covered. These Perpendicular roofs, after remaining for a period of nearly 500 years, have been destroyed within the present century. In the night of the 2nd of February, 1829, the choir was set on fire by a certain Jonathan Martin, who had hidden himself after the evening service of the previous day behind Archbishop Greenfield's tomb in the north transept. After destroying the carved stalls and the organ, the flames reached the roof, which was entirely consumed. Considerable damage was done to the stonework of the choir; and the great east window was not saved without difficulty. Martin himself (who was a brother of the well-known artist) escaped through a window of the transept, but was taken at Hexham a few days afterwards, and tried at the York assizes, when he was pronounced insane. He was confined in a lunatic asylum, and died in 1838. The cost of restoration after the fire was estimated at 65,000*l.*, which sum was raised by public subscription: 5000*l.* worth of teak timber was granted from the National Dockyards; and Sir Edward Vavasour, like his ancestors in the fourteenth century, gave the necessary stone from the Huddlestone quarries, the same which had been worked in the time of Archbishop Thoresby. The restoration, which was completed in 1832, was intrusted to Sir Robert Smirke.[*] The roof of the nave was destroyed on the 30th of May, 1840, by a fire which broke out in the south-west (the bell) tower, where some workmen had been repairing the clock. The tower was reduced to a shell; the bells were destroyed; and the flames rapidly spread to the roof of the nave, the whole of which was burnt: 23,000*l.* were raised, chiefly by subscription, for the restoration, which was completed in the following year, under the care of Sidney Smirke.

III. The cathedral is usually entered from the *south transept*, the great portal of which fronts the visitor as he enters the Minster-yard from Petergate. The transept is, as we have seen, the earliest portion of the existing church; and by commencing here, each part of the cathedral may be described in due architectural succession. (The *architecture*, the *monuments*, and the *stained glass* of each division are described separately and successively.)

Leaving the rest of the *exterior* for the present, the visitor before entering should remark that of the *south transept*. (Plate I. In this, the S.E. view of the Cathedral, the exterior of the south transept is well shown.) This transept was erected, in all probability, during the archiepiscopate of WALTER DE GRAY (1215 —1255), and is pure Early English. There is little

[*] Halfpenny's 'Gothic Ornaments in the Cathedral Church of York' is the only authentic memorial of several details of the cathedral destroyed by this fire.

PLATE I.

YORK CATHEDRAL.

YORK CATHEDRAL SOUTH-EAST VIEW.

difference in general design between the two transepts, both of which must have been completed during the lifetime of Archbishop Gray. Both have east and west aisles. The main distinction between them is in the composition of their gables, or north and south ends, which differ entirely, that of the north transept being infinitely the finer.

In the south transept the main or central portion is divided from the fronts of the aisles by enriched buttresses. Two flights of steps ascend to the portal, set in a shallow porch of very meagre composition and execution, the upper part of which is flanked on either side by a lancet-window. In the story above are three lofty pointed windows, much decorated with brackets and shafts, and with the dogtooth in their mouldings; and the actual gable is filled with a very rich rose window, with narrow pointed openings below and a triangular light above it. The pinnacle which rises at the back of the gable was not originally intended for this position, and the terminations of the buttresses are not original. A pointed arcade extends round the buttresses in the lower story, and across the aisle fronts. The upper stories of the aisle fronts have lancet windows; and three small pointed openings fill the half-gable on either side. "The lower arcade throughout this front is so miserably restored as to deprive it of half its effect: indeed, an extremely rich foliated moulding in the doorway arch is almost the only feature retaining its original beauty in the lower part of the south transept front."

The aisles east and west have large buttresses dividing each bay, with lesser buttresses between them. An arcade, intercepted by the lesser buttresses, runs round the second story. The clerestory, above the aisle roof, has an arcade of five compartments in each bay, the three central ones pierced. Above is a corbel-table of leafage. A comparison with the exterior of the north transept will show at once how far that exceeds the south in the simplicity and dignity of its general design.

IV. The view which is presented to the visitor on entering is without doubt the finest in the cathedral. (Plate II. Interior of Transept.) The great height (99 feet), breadth (93½ feet), and length (223½ feet) of the whole transept; the majesty of the fine lofty lancets which nearly fill the north gable; the solemn light struggling through their ancient diapered glass; the great central tower with its unrivalled lantern, which forms the middle distance; and perhaps to some extent the unusual point of view (since few cathedrals are entered from the transept), combine to produce an impression fully sustaining the great reputation of the Minster. It will not be for some time that the visitor will find himself capable of turning to the details of the vast building.

Each transept consists of four bays; three wider (the opening, east and west, into the aisles of nave and choir counting as one bay) and one narrow bay, the lower arches of which are walled up. In the south transept the western aisle is narrower than the

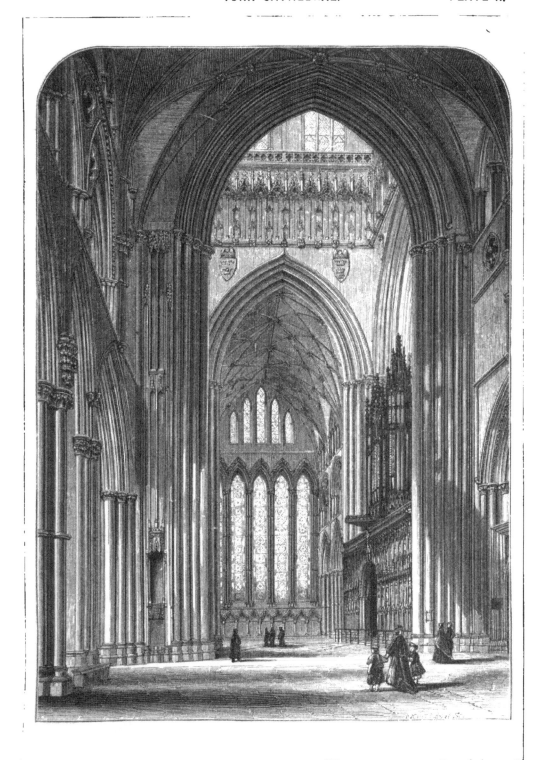

YORK CATHEDRAL. WESTERN TRANSEPT.

eastern; in the north they are of equal dimensions. The small walled-up arches, east and west, in the aisles of both transepts, adjoining the arches which open to the aisles of nave and choir, will at once attract attention. They will be better explained, however, after the transept itself has been described.

In the *south transept* the piers of the main arcades have clustered shafts, of local stone and Purbeck marble alternately. In the central piers all the shafts are ringed. In those at the ends (except that in the angles adjoining the nave, afterwards to be mentioned) only the Purbeck shafts have rings. The capitals are foliaged. The outer moulding of the main arches on the east side is enriched by a small double dogtooth ornament, with a billet between. The effect thus produced is very rich. The dogtooth occurs again on each side of the soffite; one row only being visible when the arch is looked at in front. The *triforium* in each bay is formed by a wide circular arch enriched with the dogtooth, enclosing two pointed arches, each of which is again subdivided into two. At the sides and in the centre are clustered shafts; and there are smaller ones between the lesser arches. In the main tympanum is a cusped cinquefoil, within a circle enriched with dogtooth ornament. In the lesser tympana on either side is a quatrefoil, similarly placed and enriched. In each bay of the *clerestory* is a group of five pointed arches, of equal height; the shafts between which are Yorkshire stone and Purbeck marble alternately. The arches have many mouldings, among which appears the dogtooth. At the back of the clerestory passage are three lancets in each bay, corresponding to the central arches of the arcade. The *vaulting-shafts,* in groups of three, with dogtooth ornament between them, spring from brackets of leafage between the main arches. They rise, ringed by the base moulding of the triforium, and again somewhat higher, to the crowns of the pointed triforium arches, where they terminate in capitals of leafage. On these capitals rest bases, from which triple shafts rise to the base of the clerestory, which enrings them, and forms their capitals. From the sides of the lower capitals spring circular ribbed mouldings, which pass upward to the base of the clerestory, where they terminate in tufts of leafage.

On the west side of the transept the outer mouldings of the main arches are without the double row of small dogtooth ornament, and terminate in little tufts of foliage just above the brackets of the vaulting-shafts. In the triforium there are small bosses of very good foliage below the quatrefoils in the lesser tympana, and on each side of, and below, the cinquefoil in the main tympanum.

On the south side an arcade runs on either side the door. The pointed arches spring from triple shafts, the bases of which rest on a stone plinth or seat. The capitals are foliaged; and the abacus is continued as a stringcourse quite through the arcade, at the back. Above the arcade are two pointed windows on either side of the portal, the arrangement of the wall above which deserves notice; and above again are three windows (that in the centre of two lights), set back within an arcade of pointed arches, divided by banded marble shafts, between which is the dogtooth ornament in stone. In the gable is the rose or wheel window, the best and most striking feature of this end of the transept.

It is only necessary to turn toward the north transept to perceive at once how far that gable end exceeds the south.

The wall of the west aisle is lined below the windows with a foliated arcade, having bosses of leafage at the intersections of the arches. Above, in each bay, is a pointed arcade, with shafts of stone and Purbeck marble, supporting the arches, two of which in the central bay are pierced for windows. There are two pointed windows also at the south end. Vaulting-shafts, with rich brackets, rise between each bay. In the *eastern* aisle there are five windows toward the east; and the arcade on that side is shortened, resting on a high plinth, so as to allow space for altars below it. The vaulting of both aisles is Early English. The vaulting of the main transept is a rich lierne, with many bosses. It is of wood, and is not earlier than the beginning of the fifteenth century. Until very recently the rose window in this transept, and the five smaller lancets in that opposite, were cut off by the groinings of the roof. The line of it has now been raised, so as to restore both these to the interior.

It has been asserted that the Early English foliage

—(Plate III. Corbel in South Transept)—in this and the opposite transept is a conventional representation of the Herba Benedicta (*Geum urbanum*); the trefoiled leaf of which was anciently regarded as symbolical of the Holy Trinity. It is certain that at a later period, when leafage was accurately copied from nature, the 'Herb Bennet' was extensively used in mural painting, and in other decorations; but it is very questionable whether its peculiar form can be traced in the foliage of the capitals and brackets of these transepts. At any rate, this foliage has the thoroughly conventional character and ribbed lines of the Early English period. Its arrangement, as seen in the corbel (Plate III.), is unusually varied and graceful.

V. The *stained glass* in this transept is of no great importance. That in the rose window is modern and bad. In the windows below are: in the centre, St. Peter and St. Paul; with St. William of York, east, and St. Wilfrid, west. The four lower lights are filled with glass by Peckett of York, given to the cathedral in 1793. The figures are Abraham, Solomon, Moses, and St. Peter. Here the background and accessories are thoroughly bad. In the eastern aisle is some Perpendicular glass, with the figures of St. Michael, St. Gabriel, and St. William, toward the north, in the chantry of St. Michael the Archangel, founded by Archbishop Gray in 1241 and with those of the Blessed Virgin and St. John, in the chapel founded in their honour, in 1273, by Thomas de

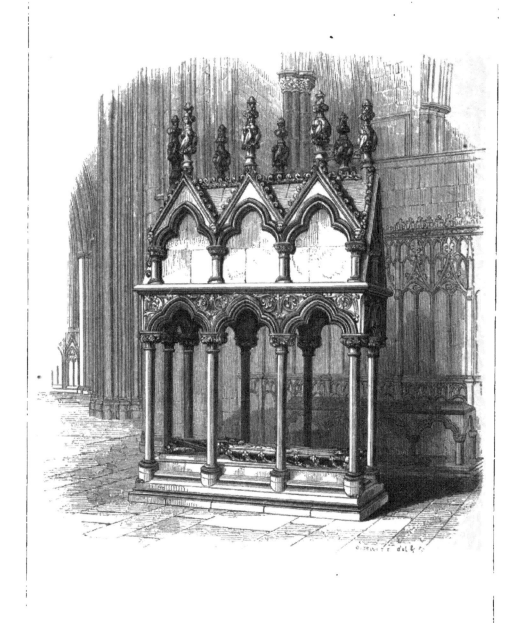

ARCHBISHOP GRAY'S MONUMENT. YORK CATHEDRAL.

Ludham, Canon of York. In the west aisle is some ancient Perpendicular glass, with modern borders. The yellow glass here used for the head of our Lord deserves notice.

VI. In the eastern aisle is the finest monument in the cathedral, the magnificent tomb (Plate IV.), with effigy and canopy, of Archbishop GRAY. (1215—1255. See Pt. II.) There is no direct evidence for assigning the foundation of the entire transept to this arch-bishop;[f] but it is certain that the transept must have been complete (or nearly so) in 1241, when he founded the chantry in which he lies interred; and it was the usual custom to bury the founder in the midst of his own work.[g]

The pier arch under which the tomb stands is made wider than the others, apparently to give it im-portance.[h] The effigy of the archbishop (who "seems to have been a man of small stature and slight frame"[i]), vested in cope, tunic, dalmatic, and alb, has an en-

[f] The tradition, however, has always run to this effect. The Antiquary Gent, writing in 1731, "mounted on his courser" to visit the little church of Skelton, near York, "because it is affirmed 'twas built with the stones that remained after the south cross of the Minster had been finished by the Archbishop Walter Gray."—Gent's 'Ripon,' pt. ii. 3. It may also be remarked, as illustrating the building propensities of Arch-bishop Gray, that the west front of Ripon was in all probability his work. (See that Cathedral.)

[g] This practice was closely followed in York Minster. "Arch-bishop Roger was buried 'in medio chori,' Archbishop Melton in the nave, at the font, and Thoresby in the Presbytery."—*Willis*, p. 21.　　　[h] Willis.　　　[i] Raine.

riched arch above the head, on either side of which are censing angels. One hand is raised in benediction; with the other the pastoral staff is held, the end of which pierces the dragon, trampled on by the feet. Over the effigy rises a lofty canopy, resting on four shafts on either side, and another at the head. These shafts have capitals of leafage, and support foliated arches, the spandrils between which are ornamented with leafage. Above, again, rises a second, smaller canopy, with three foliated arches on each side, resting on short piers with enriched capitals. This canopy is crested by gables, with heads at the intersections; and from the gables rise finials of foliage crowned by two thrushes resting upon woolpacks. The sides of the gables, and the central ridge of the canopy, have crockets of foliage.

All the details of this monument deserve very careful attention. It was retouched during the time of Archbishop Markham (1777—1807) by an Italian named Bernasconi; and the finials with their thrushes are merely of plaster.[k] These are an addition, and

---

[k] "I cannot," says Mr. Raine, "bestow too high praise on what he has done, for he seems to have been imbued with the true spirit of Christian art. He has crowned each finial with two thrushes in full song, wrought with exquisite skill, and resting upon woolpacks. Had the carving been really old I should have ventured to suggest the meaning of the device. The packs would have been an allusion to the office of chancellor, which the Archbishop once enjoyed; and in the thrushes there would have been, perhaps, a canting allusion to his name. The thrush in the North of England is at the present day frequently called the *gray bird.* It may well be singing

had no existence in the original monument. Their introduction, therefore, cannot be defended, notwithstanding their grace and beauty. The bronzed screen which surrounds the tomb was presented by Archbishop Markham, and was designed by De Corte, an artist of Antwerp. The leafage of the cresting, whether intentionally or not, resembles that attached to the shafts which support the canopy at the head of the archbishop's effigy.

East of the tomb was the altar of St. Michael, at which Archbishop Gray founded his chantry. North of the tomb is a plain marble slab, charged with a floriated cross, and elevated on low pillars. It marks the resting-place of Archbishop SEWAL DE BOVILL. (1256—1258. See Pt. II.) A gold ring, taken from the archbishop's grave, about 1735, is preserved in the vestry. It is of plain workmanship.

VII. The narrow, walled-up arches, adjoining those which open to the aisles of nave and choir, have still to be described and accounted for. It must be remembered that the Norman nave and choir remained after the erection of the Early English transepts, and that they were considerably narrower than the present ones. "It is true that the central aisle of the Norman nave was very nearly of the same width as the new one; but its side-aisles were exceedingly narrow in proportion. Each side of each transept, in accordance

—for what an offering of praise and worship is above it ! ’— ‘Lives of the Archbishops of York,’ vol. i. p. 294.

with the then existing arrangements, was provided with one *narrow* pier-arch, opposite to the side-aisle of the nave or choir, and with three other pier-arches of greater width. When the present nave was built, its wide and spacious side-aisles opened to each transept immediately against the narrow pier-arch, which had been adjusted to the narrow aisle of the preceding nave; and its pier was now found to be in the very centre of the passage from the side-aisle of the nave to the transept. As this arrangement was evidently intolerable, the pier was taken away, and a Decorated pier erected, at a greater distance from the tower-piers, so as to leave a proper space for the passage from the side-aisles to the transept. Instead, however, of constructing Decorated arches above the new pier, the Early English arches were simply shifted, and their arch-stones reset, so that at present the narrow arch which originally occupied the position nearest to each tower-pier, and corresponded to the side-aisles of the nave, is shifted to the second place; and the wide pier-arch, which originally held the second place in order from the tower-pier, has become the first in order, and serves to open the way to the side-aisles. To strengthen the building, it was also found necessary to wall up the space between these new Decorated piers and the central pier of the transept, on each side. When the choir was built, similar reasons compelled a similar change, and thus the two sides of each transept became assimilated. The triforiums, however, remained unaltered, and to this day preserve their original arrangement. They each have three wide and equal arches extending from their respective gables; and after these one narrow compartment in connexion with the tower-pier; and the clerestories, in like manner, present three equal compartments, and one narrow one; but below, reckoning from the gable, we find two wide arches, then one narrow arch, and, lastly, one wide one."[1]

It will be seen, therefore, that the piers opposite to the tower-piers, east and west, are of the same dates as the nave and choir respectively. Much dislocation is apparent in the pier adjoining the nave, and is still more visible in the opposite transept. This was caused, not by the shifting of the Early English arches, which seems to have been entirely successful, and which is accordingly characterised by Professor Willis as a "very remarkable example of the bold engineering work of the middle ages," but by the erection of the central tower, the great mass of which caused the piers on which it is raised to sink "bodily into the ground, to a depth of about eight inches," dragging with them the adjoining masonry and arches.

VIII. In its general arrangement the *north transept* resembles the south; but there are some differences of detail. It is, according to Stubbes, the work of John le Romeyn, subdean and treasurer of York (1228—1256); and its erection must have immediately followed the transept of Archbishop Gray. On the *west*

[1] Willis's 'Architectural History of York Cathedral,' p. 48.

side of this transept, the first pier from the gable end is Decorated, the original Early English pier having no doubt been removed when the narrow arch which opened to the nave was shifted. The pier of this arch, next to the tower-pier, is also Decorated. The chief points of difference between this and the corresponding side of the south transept are—the character of the foliage, which is here more advanced and natural; the smaller vaulting-shafts; and the use of a large-leafed ornament (like half a dogtooth) in the base of the triforium, and in the cornice above the clerestory. At the intersection of the main-arch moulding is an animal creeping downwards, well rendered; and above is a small figure of a saint under a Decorated canopy. On the *east* side the piers have capitals of very rich leafage, among which (in the capitals of the central pier) birds with human heads, and other grotesques, are perched. The grand and simple composition of the *north* end has been already noticed. The chief space is entirely filled by five very lofty (about 50 feet high) and narrow lancets, best known as the 'Five Sisters.'[m] These are of equal height. In the gable

---

[m] This name no doubt arose from the equal dimensions of the five windows. "There is a tradition that five maiden sisters were at the expense of these lights; the painted glass in them, representing a kind of embroidery or needlework, might perhaps give occasion for this story. This window has also been called the Jewish window, but for what reason we know not."— Gent's 'York Cathedral.' It has been suggested that the cost of this window may have been defrayed by exactions from the Jews of York.

ARCHBISHOP GREENFIELD'S MONUMENT.
YORK CATHEDRAL.

above them are five small lancets, declining from the centre. The five front windows are divided by groups of shafts, ringed in three places, and of stone and Purbeck marble alternately. The shafts which have capitals of foliage are detached, and there is a passage along the sill of the windows. The arch mouldings are enriched with dogtooth. Below, the wall is covered with a foliated arcade, resting on clustered shafts.

The 'Five Sisters' are filled with their original Early English glass, consisting of diapered patterns, varying in each window, and of very great beauty. The narrow white border which surrounds each window was inserted in 1715.[n] The glass in the five upper lancets is modern.

The small arcade in the western aisle resembles that in the opposite transept, the abacus being continuous. The vaulting has the dogtooth ornament. In the eastern aisle the wall arcade descends much lower than in the south transept, and two trefoil-headed arches, enriched with dogtooth, mark the places of altars. At the north end of this aisle a very rich decorated portal, opening to the vestibule of the Chapter-house, has been cut through the Early English work. An original Early English entrance remains at the north-east angle.

The *monuments* in this transept are—in the eastern aisle, the tomb, with canopy, (Plate V.) of Archbishop GREENFIELD (1306—1315. See Pt. II.). The very

[n] Gent.

rich canopy, which deserves notice, is crowned by a figure of the archbishop bearing his cross, and with his hand raised in benediction. This is modern, and the work of a late master-mason of the cathedral. A portion of a brass (one of the earliest existing brasses of English ecclesiastics°) remains on the tomb. The lower part was stolen about the year 1829. The archbishop is represented fully vested, and wearing the pall. A gold ring, with a ruby, taken from the tomb in 1735, is preserved in the vestry. East of the tomb stood the altar of St. Nicholas, on whose festival the death of Archbishop Greenfield occurred. It was at the back of this monument that the incendiary Martin hid himself on the night of the fire.

In this aisle is also the monument, with effigy, of Dr. Beckwith, who died in 1843, leaving to his native city the benefactions here recorded, amounting to nearly 50,000*l.*

In the west aisle is the cenotaph, with effigy, of Archbishop VERNON HARCOURT (1808—1847). The effigy, the hands of which are clasped on a book resting on the breast, is by Noble.

Behind the walled-up arch, in this aisle, is a monument called HAXEY's tomb, consisting of a flat slab, below which, enclosed by a grating, is a cadaver. Thomas Haxey was treasurer of York from 1418 until his death in 1424, and was a great benefactor to the

° The only earlier brass of an ecclesiastic which is known, is that of Richard de Hakebourne, circa 1311, in the chapel of Merton College, Oxford.—Haine's 'Manual of Brasses.'

YORK CATHEDRAL. THE NAVE, LOOKING WEST.

cathedral. He may possibly have erected this memorial (upon which, according to tradition, rents and offerings used to be paid) during his lifetime. He was himself buried a little to the south of it.[p]

IX. The Norman *nave* (Plate VI.) remained after the completion of the Early English transepts. About forty years after the death of the treasurer, John le Romeyn, the constructor of the north transept, the foundation-stone of the existing nave was laid (April 6, 1291) by his son, Archbishop Le Romeyn, or Romanus.[q] The work seems to have proceeded slowly, and with interruptions; and it was not until 1338 that the windows (including the great west window) were glazed. In 1345 the stonework seems to have been entirely complete; but the ceiling of wood was not added for ten years. Archbishop Thoresby granted the timber for it in 1355.[r] The cost of the general work was defrayed by offerings at the shrine of St. William, whose

[p] 'Fabric Rolls of York Minster' (Surtees Society), p. 206.

[q] "The dean and the canons were standing around him whilst he invoked the blessing of the Spirit on the work which was then begun (Stubbes). The Archbishop was at the south-eastern corner of the nave, hard by the transept of Walter Gray; and in front of him were the tower and the northern transept which his father had erected."—Raine's 'Archbishops of York,' vol. i. p. 340.

[r] "Vaults, whether of wood or stone, being beneath the actual roof, were not necessarily set about immediately after the building was in other respects completed, and covered in for use, but admitted of being postponed indefinitely, and indeed we often find cases in which, although prepared for, they never were added."—Willis's 'York Cathedral,' p. 29.

relics had been translated with great magnificence in 1284 ; by indulgences and briefs issued on behalf of the fabric by Archbishops Corbridge, Greenfield, and Melton ; by large contributions from the archbishops themselves ; and by grants of stone and wood from the quarries and forests of the great Northern houses, especially those of Vavasour and Percy. Archbishop Le Romeyn commenced the work at the south-east angle of the nave aisle ; and although a petition, in 1298, shows that the Norman nave had then either been pulled down or had fallen, it is probable that it was allowed to remain untouched as long as possible. The much greater width of the existing side-aisles would admit of the Norman walls standing within those of the new nave.

The nave of York Minster was thus in progress throughout the Decorated period. It can hardly be said, however, that the work, either in design or in detail, is among the best examples of English Decorated ; and, in spite of its vast dimensions, the nave of York is unquestionably inferior to those (later in date) of Winchester or Canterbury. Yet the long roofs of nave and choir, stretching away at the same great height ; the tower arches which support the lantern ; the enormous east window of the choir ; the "wall of glass" closing in the vista, and showing its upper portion above the organ-screen ; and the solemn effect of the stained glass filling the windows of nave, aisles, and clerestory ; all aid in producing an impression of grandeur which is perhaps most powerful about

halfway up the nave, where the great size and height
of the tower arch are strongly apparent, and the arcade
of the lantern, with part of its two eastern windows,
is seen. Looking westward, the great feature is the
western window, with its stately rows of saints and
archbishops. The view across the nave, through the
arch opening from the nave aisle to the transept, is
fine and unusual, owing to the great width of the aisle,
and consequently of the arch.

The design of the piers of the nave is octagonal
with attached shafts—large at the four main points,
with smaller between them. Toward the nave itself
the large shaft, with a smaller one on either side,
rise to the spring of the vaulting, somewhat above the
base of the clerestory. These shafts, the effect of
which, unbroken by ring or stringcourse, is very fine,
terminate in capitals of leafage. The capitals of the
pier shafts are also enriched with leafage, and the
outer moulding of the arches (which are very acute)
has projecting busts at its angles.

The nave has " but two great divisions; of which
the lower one, containing the pier arches, is 51 feet
high; the upper one, 43 feet high, is occupied by a
large clerestory window of five lights, with geometrical
tracery, and a transom across the middle. The lights
above the transom are glazed, and constitute the real
window; but the lights below the transom (if the
phrase can be applied to openings so perfectly dark)
are open, and as the roof of the side-aisle abuts against
the transom, the space behind them, and to which they

communicate, is the interval between the stone vault of
the aisles and its wooden roof; they thus serve the
purpose of a triforium." *   The rich and peculiar
headings of the clerestory windows should be noticed.
The triforium passage, in their high sills, is formed
by a double line of tracery, with five openings in each
bay.   In the central opening of each bay was originally
the figure of a saint.   The entire series is said to have
represented the patron saints of the different nations
of Christendom; ' but nearly all have now disappeared,
and the only remaining figure which can be identified
with any probability is that of St. George," in the fourth
bay from the west, on the south side.   From the north
bay, opposite, projects a stone beam, the head of which
is carved to represent that of a dragon.   This formerly
supported the canopy of the font.

It will be seen that the design of the nave differs
altogether from that of the transepts, and that "the
latter has not exercised the slightest influence upon
the composition of the former, although the reverse
has been frequently the case when a Decorated building

---

* Willis, p. 22.

' Gent's 'York Cathedral,' p. 48.

" Of this, however, there is some doubt.   "This figure is
commonly called St. George, but is intended, in all probability,
for a general representation of the soldier of Christ contending
with the great serpent, over against which he is placed; and
all with reference to the baptismal vow, and the Christian's
fight, of which Holy Baptism is the beginning.   The same
subject is common upon old fonts, and in other situations, and is
found long before the legend of St. George became popular."—
Poole and Hugall, p. 75.

has been added to an Early English one, as may be
seen at Ely, Westminster, and St. Alban's."[x] The
transepts have three very distinct divisions — pier-
arches, triforium, and clerestory. The nave has but
two.

In the spandrils of the pier-arches is a series of
shields, the bearings on which are probably those of
benefactors to the fabric. They are as follows, beginning at the north-east angle of the north arcade :—

1. Semé of fleur-de-lis.—Old France.

2. Six lions rampant.—Ulphus.

3. On a chevron, three lions passant guardant.—
Cobham.

4. Barry of ten, an orle of martlets.—Valence.

5. A bend, cottised, between six lions rampant.—
Bohun.

6. A fess, between six cross crosslets.—Beauchamp.

7. Quarterly, in the first quarter a mullet.—Vere.

8. A cross moliné.—Paganel.

9. Barry of ten, three chaplets.—Greystock.

10. Billetté, a lion rampant.—Bulmer.

11.
12.
13. } Three water bougets.—Roos.
14.

15. } Five Fusils in fess.—Old Percy.
16.

[x] Willis.

South-west angle of south arcade.

17.
18. } Five fusils in fess.—Old Percy.

19. Lion rampant.—Mowbray.

20. Lion rampant.—Percy.

21.
22. } Blank shields.

23. Two bars, in chief, three roundels.—Wake.

24. A fess, in chief, three roundels.—Colville.

25. On a bend, three cross crosslets.—Manley.

26.
27. } A bend.—Manley.

28. A fess dancette.—Vavasour.

29. Three chevronelles.—Clare.

30. A cross moliné.—Paganel.

31. Three lions passant guardant, with a label of three points.—Edward Prince of Wales.

32. Three lions passant guardant.—England.[y]

X. The great width (30 feet) of the *nave aisles* at once excites attention. The actual nave, or central aisle, was the same width in the Norman church as in that which now exists; but the side aisles of the Norman nave were at least 10 feet narrower. The aisle windows should be compared with the clerestory. In both "the tracery is geometrical; but in the side aisles the pattern is much simpler than in the clerestory. The former, and of course the earlier, as being lower in the building, is in three lights, without subor-

---

[y] This list, with other heraldic descriptions of shields in the fabric, is from Poole and Hugall.

dination of mouldings; but the latter is in five lights, with a rich head, and a complex subordination of mouldings."[1] Below the windows runs a very rich arcade, with gables and pinnacles; and blind arches, with similar rich headings, line the walls between the windows. The carved heads and small figures at the termination of the outer mouldings of these upper arches, should be noticed.

In the north aisle is a portal which opened to a chapel of the Holy Sepulchre, founded by Archbishop Roger, of which no remains exist. Over the door is a headless figure of the Virgin, with censing angels.

The view up these aisles, terminating at the eastern end of the choir aisles, takes in the whole length of the Minster (486 feet), and is of singular beauty.

XI. The *windows* at the west end of the nave aisles have geometrical tracery, of the same design as the others. The great *west window* of the nave itself is filled with the most exquisite flowing tracery, and in its original state was probably the work of Archbishop Melton (1317—1340), who gave a sum of 500 marks toward the completion of the west front, and who is recorded as the donor of the glass which still remains in this window. There is, however, not one old stone in it, as it was restored (precisely on the original model) many years since. The only window in England which can be considered as at all rivalling this one is the east window of Carlisle Cathedral, nearly of the

[1] Willis.

same date and character. The Carlisle window (which is the larger of the two) has been pronounced by Mr. Fergusson, "without a single exception, the most beautiful design for window tracery in the world." [a] This judgment is probably correct; but the inferiority of York is very slight, and many competent architectural critics give it the preference. "Although not the largest Decorated window in the kingdom," say Messrs. Poole and Hugall, "it is undoubtedly by far the finest, even taken without its accessories. Its great beauties are variety of design and fulness of tracery, without confusion as a whole, and without poverty of separate parts. The window at Carlisle consists of two perfect compositions, united under a common head, by the interposition of a third. That at York is one vast design, of which no part is perfect without the rest." [b] The rose window in the south transept of Lincoln Cathedral may be compared with these. "Though extremely beautiful, it wants the perfect subordination which is so satisfactory in the example at Carlisle." [c]

The great west door, below the window, displays on either side a series of niches once filled with figures. The gable was perhaps crowned by a statue of the Saviour. On either side are kneeling figures. Rows

[a] Hist. of Architecture, p. 864. "All the parts are in such just harmony the one to the other, the whole is so constructively appropriate, and at the same time so artistically elegant, that it stands quite alone, even among the windows of its own age." —*Id.*   [b] York Cathedral, p. 68.   [c] Fergusson.

of niches and blind arcading line the splays of the window. The side openings give light to the staircase of the tower.

Over the aisle doors is some curious sculpture, which deserves notice. In the north aisle is, in the centre, a woman setting her dog (which is muzzled) at two beasts, behind which is a man blowing a horn. In quatrefoils at the sides are—a man drinking, and attacked by another, and a man driving another out of his house. In the south aisle is—in the centre, a man with sword and round shield, fighting a lizard-shaped monster; and in the quatrefoils, Samson with the lion, and Delilah cutting his hair; and a man and woman·fighting. The sculpture over the door of this aisle is modern, although an exact reproduction of the old, which was greatly injured by the fire of 1840, that destroyed the roof of the nave, and began in the south-west tower.

The aisle roofs are of stone, and of the same date as the aisles themselves. The vaulting of the nave is of wood, like that destroyed in 1840. [d]

In 1863 the whole of the vast nave was fitted, for congregational purposes, with moveable benches, choir seats, and an organ by Messrs. Hill and Son. The lighting of the nave is effected by jets of gas which

[d] This vault was constructed of wood, "probably on account of the great span of the central aisle, which alarmed the masons."—*Willis.* But "the outer walls of York clerestory exhibited, before the late repairs, toothings for the reception of stone flying buttresses, which seemed to show that a stone vault was originally intended."—*Id.* p. 29, note.

form coronals round the capitals of the great piers.
In the choir a string of jets runs along at the base
of the triforium.   The Minster, thus lighted, is singularly picturesque and impressive.

XII. More than one archbishop and many other
great personages were interred in the nave; but their
monuments and brasses were entirely destroyed by the
Puritans, with the exception of a recessed tomb in
the north aisle, generally assigned to Archbishop ROGER
(1154—1181. See Pt. II.). This monument is, however,
of a much later date; although it is possible that the
remains of Archbishop ROGER may have been transferred to it from the choir, where he was originally
buried. Some bones and fragments of vestments were
found in the tomb when it was examined before its
restoration in 1862. Although the work is good, this
restoration is not to be commended; and "two birds
holding scrolls, on either side of the central figure of
the Virgin, have been metamorphosed into eagles,
with ears of wheat in their mouths."

The sainted Archbishop William of York, who died
in 1154, was then interred in the nave of the Minster,
"near the south-west pillar of the lantern."   His
remains were translated in 1284; but a tomb or cenotaph still remained in the nave, and offerings were
duly made at it. This tomb was destroyed at the
Reformation (no doubt by Dean Layton), and the
relics of the saint were replaced beneath the pavement
of the nave. Here they were discovered in 1732. (See
post, § XVI.)

Archbishop Melton (1317—1340—see Pt. II.), who contributed so largely toward the completion of the nave, was interred near the font. His coffin, in which was found a silver gilt chalice and paten, was examined during the laying down of the new pavement in 1736. This pavement is of marble and Huddlestone stone, and was designed by Kent.

XIII. The *stained glass* in the nave demands special examination and description. The glass throughout the Minster was little injured at the Reformation; and York surrendered to Fairfax in 1644, with the express stipulation that neither churches nor other buildings should be defaced. Hence the extraordinary quantity of stained glass remaining in the city.

With the exception of some Early English glass in the tracery and other parts of the clerestory windows, and of some modern in that of the aisle windows, the nave retains its original glazing—the most perfect, and perhaps the most extensive assemblage of painted glass dating from the early part of the fourteenth century of which this country can boast. Two windows in the aisles, and two in the clerestory, are alone without stained glass.

The Early English glass was possibly removed from the windows of the Norman nave, when that was demolished at the beginning of the fourteenth century. The earliest of this glass is a portion of a *Jesse* in the second window from the west, on the north side of the clerestory. "The date of the glass is about 1200. It is therefore much older than the greater part of the

Early English glass at Canterbury Cathedral, to which I do not think a date can be assigned much earlier than the middle of the thirteenth century. . . . Much Early English glass, varying in date from the beginning to the middle of the thirteenth century, has been employed to fill the wheel of tracery in the head of the last-mentioned window, as well as the wheels in the tracery of the five next clerestory windows. The upper tier of subjects in the lower lights of the fifth and seventh windows, counting from the west, on the north side of the clerestory, are also Early English. An Early English subject is inserted in one of the lower lights of the sixth clerestory window, counting from the west. The wheels in the tracery of all but three of the clerestory windows, on the south side of the nave, are likewise filled with Early English glass; and Early English glass paintings are also to be found amongst the subjects in their lower lights."[e]

The rest of the glass in the clerestory, and that in the aisles (except some modern headings) is Decorated. "The general arrangement and execution of the designs throughout this part of the building are well worthy of notice, as evincing the attention paid by our ancestors to general effects in these matters. The west windows of the nave and aisles, of which distant views may be obtained, have their lower lights filled with large figures and canopies; while the windows of the aisles, with one exception, are adorned with paint-

[e] C. Winston. "The painted glass in York Cathedral," in the York volume of the Archæological Institute.

ings of a more complicated character, and on a smaller scale, and which are therefore better calculated for a near inspection. Much of the plain geometrical glazing in the clerestory windows is original, and, like that in a similar position in Cologne Cathedral, affords a proof that the ancient glass painters did not consider themselves bound to finish patterns destined to occupy a distant position as highly as those placed nearer the eye."[t]

Much of the decorated glass in the clerestory is heraldic. The aisle windows are for the most part white pattern windows enriched with coloured pictures and ornaments. The only windows of a different character are the two westernmost in the south aisle, one of which is a Jesse, having below it the date 1789, when it was probably restored by Peckett; the other has three large and very fine figures with canopies— St. Christopher, St. Lawrence, and another saint. The earliest of the Decorated windows is probably the first (from the east) in the north aisle. This, the subject of which is the story of St. Catherine, contains many shields of arms; and from a comparison of them with a half-effaced legend across the lower part of the window, Messrs. Winston and Walford, who examined it very minutely, conclude that it was the gift of Peter de Dene, a canon of York, during the first years of the fourteenth century.[g] Many of the windows were, in

[t] Winston, *ut sup.*

[g] "On an heraldic window in the north aisle of the nave of York Minster."

all probability, special gifts to the fabric. The second bay of the north aisle (in which was the chapel of St. Thomas of Canterbury) contains a very remarkable window, which is said traditionally to have been presented by the guild of bell-founders; but which, judging from the subjects in its lower lights, seems to have been the especial gift of Richard Tunnoc, who may have been warden of the guild. He was certainly a person of considerable importance, since he had been Lord Mayor of York before his death in 1330. In the lower right-hand light of this window is shown the casting of a bell. A man blows the furnace with a pair of double bellows, on the top of which a boy is standing, pressing alternately with each foot, and supporting himself by a bar fixed above. On the opposite side of the furnace another figure, apparently Tunnoc himself, opens the furnace door with a long bent poker. The metal is seen flowing into the mould of the bell. The left-hand light shows the bell fixed in a lathe to be finished. One man turns the handle of the windlass, and Tunnoc himself applies a long turning tool, held tightly against his shoulder. His name appears above; and at the foot of this light is the inscription, "Richard Tunnoc me fist." (The legends below the other lights are too imperfect to be deciphered.) In the central light Tunnoc (with his name on a label above) is seen kneeling before an archbishop—probably Melton—who bestows his benediction. Above the figure of Tunnoc appears a small window—perhaps representing his gift. There are bells in the borders of the side lights, and in various other parts. The border of the central light represents apes playing on various musical instruments. Whether Tunnoc gave a bell to the Cathedral has not been ascertained; and it is unfortunate that the legends in this very curious window cannot be deciphered. Its upper lights contain subjects from the history of St. William of York, including the fall of the bridge. (See Pt. ii.)

The small figures of saints in the quatrefoils of the tracery in the south aisle are very fine, and should be noticed. In the west window of this aisle are figures of the Virgin, St. Catherine, and another saint. The west window of the north aisle has a Crucifixion, with the Virgin and St. John. Both these windows, the latter of which is especially striking, should be seen from the eastern end of the aisles.

The great west window was, no doubt, the last to be filled with stained glass. This was done in 1338, at the expense of Archbishop Melton, who gave 100 marks for the purpose.[h] It contains three distinct rows of figures. Below, eight archbishops, unnamed. Above, eight saints, among whom St. Peter, St. Paul, St. James, and St. Catherine are conspicuous; and above again is a series of smaller figures. The rich and solemn colouring of this window, the fine arrange-

[h] "2 Non. Feb. 1338, Magistro Thomæ Sampson vel Thomæ de Ludham custodi fabricæ eccl. B. Petri Ebor. 160 marcas pro opere vitreo fenestræ ex capite occidentali eccl. ejusdem de novo constructæ." This entry in Archbishop Melton's register was first discovered and published by the Rev. James Raine, Editor of the 'Fabric Rolls of York Minster,' p. xii. (note).

ment of figures and canopies, and the manner in which the glass is adapted to the graceful lines of the tracery, render it worthy of all possible study and attention. It should be mentioned, however, that many of the heads of the figures are modern—the work of Peckett, who was employed to restore this window about the year 1747.

XIV. Taking the Minster in chronological order, we pass from the nave into the *Chapter-house*. The erection of this, the most beautiful of English Chapter-houses,[i] has not been recorded, and the series of Fabric Rolls does not commence until long after its completion. It is certain, however, that it was in progress at the same time as the nave; and hardly less certain, from the character of its architecture, and of the stained glass which fills its windows, that it was completed before the nave,—at all events, before the west front of the nave, with its curvilinear tracery.[k]

[i] Certainly the most beautiful at present; and although the Chapter-house at Westminster, when in its perfect condition, may have almost justified the expression of Matthew Paris— " Dominus Rex ædificavit capitulum incomparabile "—it may well be doubted whether York did not exceed it in beauty. The Westminster Chapter-house, begun in 1250, is certainly earlier than that of York, whatever date is assigned to the latter. It would seem that if architectural style is to be accepted as evidence in the absence of all document, the Rev. G. Ayliffe Poole has more reason on his side than those who have taken a different view.

[k] Various dates have been assigned to the Chapter-house. Mr. Browne thinks it was begun about 1280, though not completed until far into the next century. Professor Willis is of opinion that this date " is too soon by fifty years for the beginning."—*Arch. Hist. of York*, p. 30; and his judgment is sustained by that of the Rev. James Raine, Editor of the ' York

The form of the Chapter-house, as at Wells, Salisbury, and Westminster, is octagonal; but unlike those, and unlike any except the earlier Chapter-rooms, in the form of a long parallelogram (as at Exeter, Oxford, and Chester), it has no central pillar. The vestibule opens from the north end of the transept aisle, and turns, at right angles, to the portal of the Chapter-house itself. It is clear, however, that both the north transept and the Chapter-house were completed before this vestibule was commenced. "This is demonstrable from the fact that parts of the north transept are cut away to admit of the addition of the vestibule, and that the very parapet mouldings of the Chapter-house itself appear within the vestibule which has been built against it."[1]

The solemn effect of the stained glass with which the windows of the vestibule are filled, at once impresses the visitor who passes into it from the transept. The portal has two trifoliated arches with square headings. The wall above is covered with blind tracery, resembling that of the windows. Part of the Early English buttress of the transept, a window arch, and a cornice of dogtooth above it, are here visible. Below the lofty windows of the vestibule (which resemble those of the Chapter-house—see *post*) runs a wall arcade, formed by a pointed arch enclosing two

Fabric Rolls,' Preface, p. xiv. On the other hand, Messrs. Poole and Hugall assert that the Chapter-house "does not seem more advanced than the crosses of Queen Eleanor," and suppose "that both Chapter-house and vestibule were concluded very early in the fourteenth century."—*York Cathedral*, p. 58.

[1] Poole and Hugall, p. 57.

trefoiled arches. In the tympana are, alternately, bosses of plain foliage, and human heads grotesquely encircled by foliage. The capitals of the shafts are enriched with leafage, among which are perched birds and mystical animals, including cockatrices and sphinxes. The vault is plain, with bosses at the intersections; a lozenge pattern, white on a red ground, runs along the side of the ribs. On the north side of the vestibule a doorway opens to the close.

The portal of the Chapter-house is formed by two trefoiled arches, divided by a central shaft. These arches are circumscribed by a main arch with a quatrefoil in the tympanum, containing two brackets for figures. In a niche against the central shaft is a mutilated figure of the Virgin and Child of extreme beauty. The Purbeck marble of the shafts is fast decaying, whilst the Yorkshire stone is still perfectly sound. The Chapter-house retains its original oaken door, covered on the interior with a kind of trellis-work of wood, and on the exterior with scrolled iron-work, deserving the closest attention. The scrolls, which are cut into leafage and flowers, are admirable in design, and terminate at the top of the doors in dragons and lizard-like monsters. They should be compared with the ironwork of the cope chest in the choir aisle, which is of the same date. (See post, § xix.) It is said that four of these chests stood originally in the centre of the Chapter-house.

3000l. of the sum left to the Minster by the late Dr. Beckwith, whose monument is in the transept, were appropriated by him to the restoration of this Chapter-house. This was accordingly commenced in 1844. Much of the Purbeck marble was then renewed. The vault was restored and decorated by Willement, and the floor was laid with Minton's tiles. All traces of the ancient painting and gilding were then unhappily obliterated; but no amount of restoration has as yet deprived this building of its right to stand at the head of English Chapter-houses. It is still fully entitled to the distinction implied in the ancient verse painted on the left side of the entrance—"Ut Rosa flos florum sic est domus ista domorum."

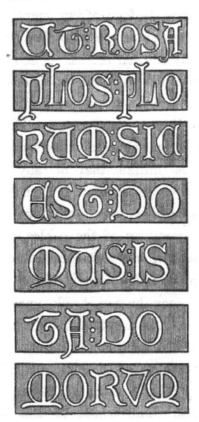

These letters have been carefully traced from the original.

Each bay of the Chapter-house (Plate VII.) contains a lofty window, with magnificent geometrical tracery of somewhat late character. Each circle in the headings has nine cusped foliations. Below runs an arcade of wonderful beauty. There are six arches in each bay; and each arch contains a recessed semi-octagonal seat, with attached shafts of Purbeck marble at the angles and at the back. In front of each angle rises an entirely detached shaft of the same marble. Each seat is groined, with a boss of hollow-worked leafage in the centre, and the capitals of the Purbeck shafts are worked in varied leafage of ivy, maple, oak, and other trees. The overhanging canopy has two pendants of leafage in front of each recess. The canopy, which is gabled, is enriched with finials of oak-leaves; and a cornice of vine-leaves and grapes bends round above it, following the line of the recesses. The effect of this superb mass of enrichment is perhaps unique. The arrangement is unlike that of any other English Chapter-house, especially in the form of the seats, and in that of the cornice above the canopy.

At the intersections of the gables, and at the angle between each stall, are grotesque heads and figures of wonderful spirit and variety. Besides animals and birds, there occur human heads, men fighting with monsters and with each other, besides several monastic figures, full of the satire in which the secular clergy were always ready to indulge. Birds and small animals are perched among the leaves of some of the pendent bosses. The whole of this sculpture will

YORK CATHEDRAL CHAPTER HOUSE.

PLATE VII

repay the very closest examination. It is distinguished
by that careful imitation of Nature which belongs to
the work of the early part of the fourteenth century ;
and in the spirit of the heads and grotesques, and the
graceful arrangement of leafage, it is exceeded by no
other sculpture of this period, either in England or
on the Continent.[m]

The entrance portal should be examined from the
interior. Above it is a wall arcade of very beautiful
design, with thirteen brackets for figures of the Saviour
(or the Virgin and Child) and the Apostles. These—
which are traditionally said to have been of silver
gilt—have disappeared. Two angels remain at the
sides above. A wall passage, with square-headed openings in the splays, runs round below the windows of
the Chapter - house. Between each bay, clustered
vaulting shafts run to the roof, which is of wood. The
vaulting ribs pass to a central boss, on which is the
Lamb bearing a flag with a cross. This is modern.
The roof, before the restoration in 1845, was " richly
painted with the effigies of kings, bishops, &c., and
large silver knots of carved wood at the uniting of the
timbers, all much defaced and sullied by time."[n]

[m] The whole of this sculpture was one mass of gilding and
colour, the traces of which were removed in 1844. On the wall
above the entrance were three full-length figures, an Archbishop
between a King and Queen, possibly Archbishop Melton
between Edward II. and his Queen Isabella.

[n] Gent's ' York Cathedral,' p. 15. The wooden vaulting is
firmly connected with the principal timbers. There was a
tradition, says Gent, that during the Commonwealth " a certain

The stained glass with which the windows are filled adds not a little to the solemnity of the building. They are white windows with coloured medallions, and shields in the tracery, some of which are modern. All this glass "is of the time of Edward II. and commencement of the reign of Edward III., and is an extremely beautiful specimen of early Decorated work.° The east window is alone modern, and the work of Messrs. Barnett, of York. "If it does not produce so satisfactory an effect as the original windows, this arises not from the fault of the artist, but from the impossibility of procuring at the present day a material similar in texture to the glass of the fourteenth century."ᵖ The subjects in this window are from the Life of our Lord. The borders of the ancient windows, and all the details of the glass, afford admirable studies and examples, and should be carefully examined. The windows in the vestibule are of the same date, and consist chiefly of single figures under canopies. Some Early English glass, of the same character and date as that in the "Five Sisters" (in the north transept), has been inserted in the tracery of the second window from the door, in the vestibule.

Some panels of the old ceiling of the Chapter-house (removed in 1844) are preserved here. On one of them appears the Jewish Church, blindfolded, her

person obtained a grant to pull down the Chapter-house as a useless part of the church." This he would have done "had not death surprised him a week before the intended execution of his wicked project."   ° Winston.   ᵖ Ibid.

O. JEWITT. del. & sc.

YORK CATHEDRAL. THE CHOIR.

crown falling, and the reed broken on which she leans.

XV. Leaving for the present the central tower and the rood-screen, we pass into the *Choir* (Plate VIII.). After the completion of the nave, it was determined to replace Archbishop Roger's late Norman choir with one of greater size and magnificence; and, whilst so doing, to provide a place "where the mass of the Blessed Virgin might be fittingly celebrated." Archbishop Roger's choir had short eastern transepts, and terminated, eastward, two bays beyond them. The design for the new work extended it three bays towards the east, and widened the whole choir and presbytery by making the aisle walls run in a line, east and west, with the outer walls of the short Norman transepts. The Presbytery and Lady Chapel, forming the four easternmost bays of the existing building, were first completed,[q] and it is probable that until their completion the Norman choir was not interfered with, and was still available for service. Afterwards, this choir was entirely removed, and that which now exists was

[q] The term "Presbytery" is here used, as it has been by Professor Willis and others who have written on the Minster, to denote the four easternmost bays of the building, including the Lady Chapel. But, strictly speaking, no part of this was ever included in the true Presbytery, which is the part of the church between the "Chorus cantorum," and the high altar, set apart for the clergy who are ministering at the latter. At York, before the Reformation, and indeed long afterwards, the high altar stood at the eastern end of the *fifth* bay; so that what is here called the Presbytery was behind it, and formed the retrochoir with its aisles.

continued from the new Presbytery, until it joined the Early English transepts and the central tower.

The first stone of the new Presbytery was laid on the 30th of July, 1361, by Archbishop Thoresby (1352—1373), who had already granted timber for the completion of the ceiling of the nave, and had been otherwise a considerable benefactor to the fabric. The Presbytery is, however, his especial memorial. Toward its construction he gave the stone of his manor-house at Sherburn, which had fallen into decay,[r] besides a yearly sum of 200*l.* during the remainder of his life. The amount of Archbishop Thoresby's contribution towards this part of the Minster cannot be estimated, "in the money of the present day, at a lower sum than 37,000*l.*, and this, in all probability, is considerably under the mark."[s] Large additional sums were raised by grants of indulgence to all bene-factors, by taxes laid on the Chapter clergy, and by subsidies levied on the church property throughout the diocese. Brief-bearers (brevigeri) were also sent through the country to beg for the fabric.[t] The Presbytery was accordingly completed before the death of Thoresby in 1373, within twelve years from its com-

---

[r] See the grant in the 'Fabric Rolls of York Minster,' p. 174.

[s] Raine's 'Archbishops of York,' i. p. 484. The payment of the annual grant is confirmed by the Archbishop's Register.— *Id.* note.

[t] They were sent into other dioceses. The form of brief for those in the diocese of Lincoln is given in the 'Fabric Rolls,' p. 178.

mencement. After his death the work remained for
some time at a standstill, owing apparently to the loss
of the archbishop's large donations, and to the troubles
of his successor, Alexander Neville (1374—1388), who
was an exile from York during the greater part of
his episcopate. The choir seems to have been commenced about the year 1380, and in 1385 the Chapter
obtained a lease of the quarry of Huddlestone for
eighty years,ᵘ showing that they were in want of stone,
and that the work was in progress. The walls were
completed about 1400,ᵛ and the roof and wooden vaulting were finished at the beginning of 1405.ˣ

The Choir and Presbytery thus completed were perhaps the most magnificent works which, up to this
date, had been attempted in England; and it is quite
possible, as has been suggested by Mr. Raine, that
William of Wykeham, at Winchester (1367—1404),
and Walter Skirlaw, at Durham (1388—1405), both
of whom were connected with the church of York, and
were intimate friends of Archbishop Thoresby, were
encouraged to undertake great architectural works in,

ᵘ 'Fabric Rolls,' 13 (note). Some Huddlestone stone occurs
in the Presbytery; but this no doubt came from the manor-
house at Sherburn. There is no evidence to show that the
Chapter had any right over that famous quarry until 1385.

ᵛ So it would appear from a fabric roll of 1399, in which
great preparations are recorded for gathering together timber
and other materials for the roof.—*Fabric Rolls*, p. 13.

ˣ So Mr. Raine argues from a fabric roll of 1404; in which is
a "charge for plastering the walls and the altars in the new
choir. Now this would not be done till the roof was safely
upon the walls."—*Ib.*, p. 24, note.

E

and connected with, their own cathedrals by the beautiful structure " they would gaze upon as it rose from the ground at York."[y] The visitor, on entering the choir, is first struck by the great eastern window, the largest in England that retains its original glazing (see *post*, § xviii.), the lower part of which is seen through the pierced altar-screen. This superb " wall of glass," rich in design and colour, and the stained windows, of equal height, filling the ends of the transept bays ; the lofty clerestory lights, also masses of solemn colour ; the double plane of the triforium passage below producing grand effects of light and shade ; and, above all, the vast height (102 feet) and width (99½ feet) of the choir, impress the mind with a sense of grandeur, which steadily increases as the building becomes better known. Other English choirs are more picturesque ; none is more majestic than this of York.

The general design of both choir and presbytery repeats that of the nave. There are two great divisions, the lower containing the pier arches, the upper the clerestory, the high sills of which form the triforium passage. The four easternmost bays (three of them beyond the present altar screen) forming the presbytery and Lady Chapel, completed during Thoresby's episcopate, although they agree in general character with the actual choir, exhibit in their details very distinct evidence of their earlier date. Standing toward the upper end of the choir, where the clerestory of both choir and presbytery may be seen at once, the

    y Raine's ' Lives of the Archbishops of York,' i. 482.

contrast pointed out by Professor Willis will be at once clear. The clerestory windows were no doubt intended to match. "The number of lights are the same in each, and so is the system of subordination, by which two lights on each side are cut off, and included in a separate arch. (This, indeed, is also derived from the nave.) But in the presbytery a transom crosses the tracery, and connects these arches. In the choir, on the contrary, the two central monials run up with decided Perpendicular character to meet the window arch. In the presbytery, these monials run up, but in the subordinate order of mouldings only, so as not to be prominent. The head of the presbytery window is occupied by a series of compartments that recline right and left fan-wise, and have many flowing lines in them, strangely mixed with others of decided Perpendicular character. But in the choir the whole of the filling up is of the most decided Perpendicular character, and shows that when this part of the building had been reached, the Perpendicular style had become fully established."[z] Other differences between the presbytery and choir are that "in the presbytery the monials of the clerestory have *long* cylindrical base plinths, and *trefoiled* compartments between them at the bottom of the triforium. The capitals of the triforium arches also *embrace the small outer shafts* of the window arch. The transom of the triforium openings is rather *higher* than the middle. In the choir, on the contrary, there are *short* plinths with

[z] Willis's 'Architectural History of York Cathedral,' p. 25.

cinquefoil compartments between the capitals; the latter *stop short* of the outer shafts, and the transom is *lower down*."[a] In the presbytery the clerestory passage runs outside the windows; in the choir, within the glass.

The small heads which terminate the outer mouldings of the pier arches, and the general design of capitals and foliage, are imitated from the nave. On the north side of the choir, however, the capitals of the piers have some figures inserted among the foliage which deserve notice. Mr. Browne has found in them "the principal events of the tragedy which ended in the death of Archbishop Scrope." But the choir was no doubt completed before his death in 1405; and there is no authority whatever for the appropriation.

Against each pier of the presbytery is a bracket and enriched canopy. These do not appear in the choir proper; but two of them, happily unrestored, remain on the piers adjoining the altar-screen. In the spandrils of the main arches of both choir and presbytery are shields of arms, slung from turbaned heads. They are chiefly those of benefactors, and of other persons connected with the cathedral. These, commencing at the north-east end of the north arcade, are as follows :—

1. Two keys in saltire.—Chapter of York.

2. Six lions rampant.—Ulphus.

3. Three lions passant guardant, a label of three points, each point charged with three fleur-de-lis.— Thomas, Duke of Lancaster.

[a] Willis, p. 25.

4. Three lions passant guardant, a border.—Edmund of Woodstock.

5. A bend between six lions rampant.—Bohun.

6. Checky, a fess.—Clifford.

7. A cross floré.—Latimer.

8. Barry of ten, three chaplets.—Greystock.

9. The Instruments of the Passion.

10. Three estoiles of six points, a border.—St. Wilfred.

11. Two keys in saltire, a border engrailed.—St. Peter.

12. Two swords in saltire, a border engrailed.—St. Paul.

13. Seven lozenges conjoined, 3, 3, and 1.—St. William Archbishop.

14.—On a bend, a lion rampant.—Musters.

15. A chief, three chevronelles interlaced in base.—Fitz-Hugh.

16. On a saltire, a crescent.—Neville.

17.
18.} A fesse dancette.—Vavasour.

South arcade, commencing at the west :—

1. A cross.—St. George.

2. A cross floré between five martlets.—Edward the Confessor.

3. Three crowns, 2 and 1.—King Edwin.

4. Barry of six, on a chief, two pallets between as many esquires, based.—Mortimer.

5. Six lions rampant; 3, 2, 1, with a horn on the west side of the shield (referring to the famous gift of lands).—Ulphus.

6. A lion rampant.—Percy.

7. Quarterly, 1 and 4, a lion rampant, for Percy; 2 and 3, three luces hauriant, for Lucy.—Percy.

8. A bend, a label.— Scrope of Masham.

9. Six osier wands interlaced in cross.—Bishop Skirlaw.

10. A bend, a border charged with mitres, over all a label.—Archbishop Scrope.

11. Three water bougets.—Roos.

12. A saltire.—Neville.

13. On a cross, five lions passant guardant.—City of York.

14. Three fusils in fesse.—Montague.

15. A fesse between six cross crosslets.—Beauchamp.

16. A lion rampant.—Percy.

17. France (ancient) and England quarterly, with a label of three points.—Edward Prince of Wales.

18. France (ancient) and England, quarterly.

XVI. The fire of 1829 destroyed, as has already been mentioned, all the wood-work of the choir, including the roof, which was of wood, like that of the nave. The present vault is an exact reproduction of that which formerly existed, and is a very rich lierne. The stalls are also close copies of the old ones; and considering that the restoration under Sir R. Smirke was effected before the revival of Gothic architecture, it is highly creditable. The original stone altar-screen was destroyed by the fall of heavy beams, and by the general effect of the fire; but that which has replaced it is of very great beauty, and "so perfect a restoration that it may be treated as a study of Perpendicular screen-work."[b] (See it in Plate VIII., *ante*.) The altar now stands immediately in front of this screen. Until the year 1726, however, it stood one bay further westward; and at its back was a wooden reredos, rising very high, so as to obstruct the view of the east window, "handsomely painted and gilt, with a door at each end" opening into the space between it and the stone screen. On the top of the reredos was a music gallery. The space behind it is said to have served as a vestry " where the archbishops used to robe themselves at the time of their enthronisation;[c] but it seems to have been so prepared for the enthronisation alone of Archbishop Kempe in 1427; and Professor Willis suggests that it was in all probability the place where the portable feretrum or shrine of St. William was kept.[d] On the removal of the wooden reredos by Dean Finch in 1726, the altar was placed in its present position.

The sainted Archbishop William of York (1143—1154, for a sketch of his life see Pt. II.) was interred

[b] Poole and Hugall. Archbishop Lamplugh (1688–1691) hung the original screen with " three pieces of fine tapestry," representing the finding of Moses, the rain of manna, and Moses smiting the rock. In 1760 Dean Fountayne removed this tapestry, and filled the arches with plate glass (Gent's ' York '), an arrangement which has been repeated in the present screen.

[c] Drake's 'Eboracum,' p. 523. Gent's ' York Minster,' p. 45.

[d] ' Architectural History of York Cathedral,' p. 53. The position of the feretory, or " holy hole," at Winchester may be compared.

at first in the nave of the minster; but on the 8th of January, 128¾, his remains were translated by Archbishop Wickwaine, in the presence of Edward I.,[e] his Queen Eleanor, and a great company of prelates and nobles. The cost of translation was defrayed by Antony Bek, "le plus vaillant clerk de roiaume," who on the same day was consecrated to the see of Durham.[f] The relics were borne into what was still the Norman choir of Archbishop Roger; and on the completion of the existing choir they no doubt found a resting-place in the position assigned to the shrine by Mr. Willis. The shrine itself was richly decorated; and the head of the saint was kept by itself in a reliquary of silver, gilt, and covered with jewels. Layton, Henry VIII.'s commissioner, who was Dean of York, obtained a special grant of this reliquary for the use of the cathedral.[g] The relics of St. William

[e] "The King had recently fallen from an eminence, and had escaped unhurt. He ascribed his good fortune to the agency of St. William, and hastened to York to show his gratitude by being present at the translation of his body."—Raine's *Lives of the Archbishops of York*, i. p. 228; where will be found a minute and interesting account of the translation from the York Breviary.

[f] Three years and a half before, on the Octave of St. Michael, 1280, Thomas Bek, brother of Antony, translated at his own expense the remains of St. Hugh of Lincoln, and on the same day was consecrated, in Lincoln Cathedral, to the bishopric of St. David's. Edward I. and Queen Eleanor were also present on this occasion. (See 'Lincoln Cathedral,' Part II.). Bishop Thomas Bek was now with his brother at York.

[g] "This head was the greatest treasure that the church of York possessed. When Margaret, daughter of Henry VII.,

seem to have been interred at this time near their ancient resting-place in the nave; where in May, 1732, Drake, the historian of York, found a leaden box containing "a number of bones huddled carelessly together without any order or arrangement."[h] Until the Reformation, this original place of sepulture seems to have been marked by a cenotaph at which offerings were made, as well as at the shrine itself.

The eagle lectern in the choir was the gift of Dr. Cracroft in 1686. For the stained glass in the clerestory windows, see *post*.

XVII. The *aisles* exhibit the same differences as the choir and presbytery; the four easternmost bays being of the earlier date; the transeptal bay, with those westward of it, of the later. The windows of the eastern bays are more acutely pointed than the others; and their tracery is less distinctly Perpendicular, for, "although the pattern traced out by the first lines, or first order of tracery mouldings, is a kind of reticulation that not unfrequently occurs in early Perpendicular windows; yet the way in which each of the meshes (so to speak) of this reticulation above the lights is filled up, has a decidedly flowing character, which is given to it by the inclination to right and left of the trefoiled compartments, and by

visited the minster, the head was brought for her to kiss."—Raine's *Archbishops*, p. 330, note.

[h] *Id.* There was a tradition that the relics had been interred here; and the search was made by Drake when the existing pavement of the nave was laid down.

their flowing junction with the quatrefoil above them." [1]
The windows are of three lights each; and the slender
shafts with enriched capitals, dividing the lights,
should be noticed, as adding to the effect. The wall
spaces between the windows are divided by a group of
vaulting shafts, on either side of which are two
ranges of broad, canopied niches, with pedestals for
statues. Below runs a plain arcade, lining the wall.
The vaulting shafts, which terminate above in capitals
of foliage, have lower capitals, or rings of leafage, at
the top of the arcade string-course. The vaulting
itself (of stone) is plain, with small leaf bosses at the
intersections.

The easternmost bay of each aisle is narrower than
the others, and the side windows have only two lights.
The eastern windows are of three, and in no way differ
from the rest. At the angles (north-east and south-
east) are doors opening to staircases which lead up-
wards to a passage through the base of the eastern
aisle windows, and thence ascend to the galleries in
front of the great east window of the presbytery. At
the east end of the north aisle was the altar of St.
Stephen; at the end of the south, the altar of All
Saints.

The lesser or eastern transepts (which do not
project beyond the aisles, and should rather be called
transeptal bays) belong to the second period—that in
which the choir was erected. They represent, in effect,

---

[1] Willis, p. 24.

the transeptal towers of Archbishop Roger's Norman
choir (see § xxiii.);[k] and may be reckoned among the
most original features of the minster. "The exquisite
and unique effect of the tall windows, rising almost
from the floor into the roof, and occupying the whole
width of the transept, is beyond all praise; it is one
of those felicitous efforts of architectural skill in which
the creative genius of a master-hand is recognised."[1]

The lower part of the window (like the great east
window) has a double plane of tracery; the inner,
or open lights being exactly similar to those in
which the glass is fixed. At each side of the window
are, above, three rich canopies and brackets; and
below, two lesser ones, like those of the aisle windows.
A lofty arch opens from the transept, east and west;
and another of the same height opens to the choir.
Above this arch the triforium gallery passes. A
second arch, with side shafts, level with the clerestory

[k] The choir of York minster, as restored or rebuilt by the
first Norman Archbishop Thomas (1070–1100), was short and
apsidal. Archbishop Roger (1154–1181) took it down, and
rebuilt it of much greater size, and on a different plan. This
late Norman choir had a square eastern end, and short eastern
transeptal towers, the foundations of which remain in the
crypt. Before his elevation to the see of York, Roger had been
Archdeacon of Canterbury; and many peculiarities of the
"glorious choir of Conrad" in that cathedral (completed 1130,
destroyed by fire 1174), were imitated at York. Among them
was the double transept. Canterbury, however, had towers
flanking the choir, north and south, as well as a second or
eastern transept. At York the flanking towers were made to
perform the part of transepts also.

[1] Poole and Hugall.

windows, rises from the gallery to the roof, and through it the upper part of the transept window is visible from the choir. Above the arches, east and west, is a window of the same height as the clerestory.

At the spandrils of the arches are shields of arms. In the

North transept, east side—

1. A chief, three chevronelles interlaced in base—Fitz-Hugh.

2. A bend, a label of three points — Scrope of Masham.

North side—

1. Three escallopes—Dacres.

2. A fess between six cross crosslets—Beauchamp.

West side—

1. On a saltire, a martlet—Neville.

2. A bend—Scrope of Masham.

South side—

1. Checky, a fess—Clifford.

2. A cross floré—Latimer.

South transept, east side—

1. A lion rampant—Mowbray.

2. A lion rampant—Percy.

West side—

1. A fess dancette—Vavasour.

2. A blank shield.

North side—

1. A fess between three cross crosslets — Beauchamp.

2. Three escallopes—Dacres.

XVIII. The general character of the so-called presbytery, or *retrochoir*, has been already described. The
canopies against the piers, and those under the east
window, should be remarked and compared. The
stone carving in this part of the cathedral was greatly
injured by the fire of 1829 ; and five of the canopies
against the piers " were renewed by John Scott, the
minster mason ; when changes were very injudiciously
admitted into them. The wanton alteration, even of a
minute feature, must always be deprecated in such
instances. . . . There is less difference between the
two ends of the choir, at an interval of nearly fifty
years from one another, than has been wantonly
produced between canopies on adjoining pillars, whose
place in the history of the church is identical." [m] The
original canopies, unrestored, remain on the piers
adjoining the altar-screen.

The great east window—(see its general character
in Plate VIII. *ante*)—the largest window in the kingdom that retains its original glazing[n]—is one of the
chief glories of the minster, and is best examined
here. It is impossible to look up at it without
feelings of increasing wonder and admiration. In

[m] Poole and Hugall., p. 109.

[n] The east window of Gloucester Cathedral is somewhat larger,
but is partially (in the lower part) unglazed. The Gloucester
window is about 72 ft. high, and 38 wide. The York window,
which is entirely glazed, about 78 ft. high and 33 wide. It should
be remembered that these enormous windows are peculiar to
England. The York and Gloucester windows are therefore the
largest in the world.

itself the design is fine and unusual. Almost filling the entire bay, the window rises quite to the roof, in three lofty stages, the two lower having an inner plane of open arches, through which, at the base, runs a passage, with doors at the angles opening to a staircase in the buttress turrets of the window, by which access is gained to a second gallery, with a parapet in front, running across at the foot of the highest stage. The elaborate tracery which fills the upper part of the window is of the same undecided character (Perpendicular with some flowing details) which has already been noticed in the windows of the clerestory and aisles. The jambs of the window, in each stage (within the plane of open arches) were enriched with figures, for which the brackets and canopies remain. The under part of the gallery is covered with panelled tracery. Above, in the window jambs, are heads of saints, with canopies, arranged at intervals; and small canopied brackets, with figures of angels, form a continuous outer moulding.

The narrow wall space on each side of the window has a double row of brackets, with canopies, ascending in four tiers. Under the window the wall is lined with a plain arcade, nearly hidden by monuments. In the centre, above the place of the altar, are three canopied niches. At the base are figures of angels, kings, and bishops; all deserving examination.

The view from the upper gallery of this window is very striking. The west window of the nave, especially, is best seen from this place.

Beneath this window was the altar of the Lady-chapel, founded by Archbishop Thoresby, and before which he was himself interred, in the midst of the magnificent building he had so largely assisted in raising.° The remains of several of the archbishop's predecessors, removed from the Norman choir, were re-interred here, under monuments which were made for them at Thoresby's expense.ᵖ These formed a series of brasses, the greater part of which were destroyed during the Civil War; and the rest (with

° Mr. Browne ('History of York Minster') has endeavoured to prove that the Lady-chapel built by Thoresby was on the north side of the nave, and that he was interred there. Professor Willis, however, and Mr. Raine ('Fabric Rolls' and 'Lives of the Archbishops of York') show conclusively that Thoresby's Lady-chapel was at the east end of the choir. The chronicler Stubbes declares that Thoresby finished this chapel, and removed to it the bodies of his predecessors. Leland describes the tombs of six archbishops, Thoresby among them, at the east end of the church, "in orient. parte ecclesiæ" ('Itin.' viii. 14), and the antiquary Torre, at the end of the 17th century, measured these tombs, marked their places in his map of the pavement, and sketched them in pen and ink. A copy of this sketch (which shows distinctly that the tombs were those of archbishops) is inserted by Mr. Raine in his preface to the 'Fabric Rolls,' p. xviii. The chain of evidence is thus complete.

ᵖ "1368-9, 13 Feb., Magistro Roberto de Patrington magistro cementario fabricæ chori eccl. nostræ Ebor. Super opere sex lapidum marmoreorum pro tumulis predecessorum nostrorum parandis de quibus secum convenimus 10*l.*; 1369, 23 Aug. eidem 10 marcas in partem solucionis 40*l.* pro factura quorundam lapidum marmoreorum. 1373, 12 Jun. eidem 100*s.* argenti pro opere tumbarum."—Thoresby's *Register*, ap. Raine's *Fabric Rolls*, Preface, xv., note.

the stones containing the matrices) disappeared when the choir was newly paved.

XIX. Of the *monuments* in the *north* aisle of the choir and presbytery, the most remarkable are as follows:—In the last bay of the aisle, westward, and against the wall of the transept aisle, is a high tomb, recessed, with the effigy of WILLIAM OF HATFIELD, second son of Edward III., born 1336; died 1344; aged 8. The effigy is finely wrought. The Prince wears a short tunic, covered with a rich leaf ornament, and a mantle, the border of which is foliated. The shoes are diapered; and the flowing hair is bound with a small coronet. The face is much broken. In the front of the high tomb are two panels of peculiar tracery. The canopy above and behind the figure has been powdered with the *plantagenista*.[q] The fact that one of her children was interred in the minster probably accounts for the gift of a richly embroidered bed belonging to Queen Philippa, which was made to the chapter either by the Queen herself or by Archbishop Thoresby.[r]

On the south side of the aisle is the monument, with effigy, of Archbishop SAVAGE (1501—1507). The very rich mitre deserves notice. The frieze with angels bearing shields, and the hollowed recesses at

---

[q] This was first pointed out by Mr. Raine, 'Lives of the Archbishops of York,' i. p. 422, note. The effigy had been removed to another part of the church, and was restored to its present position by the poet Mason when he was precentor.

[r] 'Fabric Rolls,' p. 125; Raine's 'Archbishops,' i. p. 422.

the sides indicate the lateness of the work. In the
next bay is the entrance to the crypt. In front stand
two large cope chests, said to have been brought from
the chapter-house. They are of the fourteenth century, and the flowing iron-work with which they are
covered should be compared with that on the chapter-
house doors.

Beyond the transept, the arcade lining the wall below
the windows is nearly hidden by heavy monuments
of the seventeenth and eighteenth centuries. The first
is that of Sir HENRY BELLASIS, without a date, but
about 1630. Beyond are—MARGARETTA BYNG, "Lon-
dinensis; ter vidua, pia, honesta, proba," in very rich
ruff and dress, kneeling before a desk; 1600. Sir
WILLIAM INGRAM and wife, 1625; half figures under a
canopy, gilt and coloured. Sir William was " of the
King's Council in the North." CHARLES HOWARD, Earl
of Carlisle, died 1684; ambassador (1663, 4) to Russia,
Sweden, and Denmark. Admiral MEDLEY, died 1757;
with bust and weeping cherubs; Dr. DEALTRY, died
1773, with a figure of Hygeia lamenting, and some
edifying verses below. Sir GEORGE SAVILE, died 1784;
a full-length by Fisher of York. Sir George represented the county of York in parliament for twenty-five
years, and the statue was erected by public subscription. Dr BREARY, Prebendary of York, died 1735;
with an inscription recording his descent and connec-
tions; and LIONEL INGRAM, a boy of two years old,
son of Sir Arthur Ingram, with a remarkable Latin
epitaph; a very good example of a small Jacobæan

F

monument. At the end of the aisle, under the window, is the monument of Archbishop STERNE (1664—1683. See Pt. II.). The archbishop, robed and mitred, is under a canopy, looped up at the sides; and is supported by very ugly cherubs.

Adjoining is the plain tomb of Frances Cecil, Countess of Cumberland; died 1643.

XX. In the *presbytery* the monuments are—In the bay between the aisle and the Lady-chapel, Archbishop SCROPE (1398; beheaded, 1405, June 8). This is a plain tomb, restored after the fire of 1829. (See Pt. II.) Such was the indignation felt throughout Yorkshire at Scrope's "legalised murder," that his virtues—(which were in truth not small, he was a man of letters and of a "holy life")—became magnified, in popular estimation, to an extraordinary degree, and his tomb here was sought by thousands as that of a saint. Offerings were made at it, and miracles were said to have occurred before it. The offerings were forbidden by an order from the King, Henry IV.,* and the officers of the cathedral were directed to pull down the screen (clausure de charpenterie) which surrounded the monument, and to pile wood and stone over the tomb (between the pier and the east wall), so as to prevent the access of the people.† The order was not, however, strictly obeyed.

---

* This order to the Chapter, from Arundel, Archbishop of Canterbury, and Thomas Langley, Dean of York and Chancellor of England—confirmed by the King,—is printed in Raine's 'Fabric Rolls,' p. 194.

† "Et y faces mettre sur la terre entre les pilers et par bonne espace de hors veilles fuystes et grosses piers de bonne hautesse

Offerings continued to be made ; and at the Reformation the treasures of St. Stephen's Chapel (adjoining the tomb, on the north side), in which they were deposited, were among the richest in the cathedral.[u] The Scropes had their chantry there, and many of the archbishop's ancestors had been interred in this chapel. At the same time with Archbishop Scrope were buried in the minster (where is not known) Thomas Mowbray, Duke of Norfolk, and Sir John Lamplugh, both of whom were beheaded on the same charges.

Under the next bay, between the presbytery and the aisle, is the cenotaph of Archbishop Markham (1777—1807), buried in Westminster Abbey. The top is a slab of black marble, inlaid with a cross, and the inscription, "Equidem ego novi redemptorem meum vivere." At the sides are shields of arms.

The altar platform of the Lady-chapel is raised on two steps. Under the east window are :—

(1.) Towards the north, Archbishop ACCEPTED FREWEN (1660—1664) in cap, rochet, and black gown.

(2.) Against the wall, FRANCES MATTHEW, wife of Archbishop Matthew, died 1629. She was the daughter of William Barlow, Bishop of Chichester, and one of four sisters, all of whom married bishops.

(3.) Archbishop SHARPE (1691—1714), reclining, with a book in his left hand ; below is a long inscription.

. . . . pour faire estoppoil à les faux foles que y veignont par couleur de devocion."—*Fabric Rolls*, p. 196.

[u] Raine's 'Fabric Rolls,' p. 194, note.

In front, and projecting over the steps, are:—

(1.) Towards the north, Archbishop ROTHERHAM (1480—1500), a perpendicular high tomb, with quatre-foils at the sides, and white marble drapery spread over the top. The tomb was restored after the fire by Lincoln College, Oxford, of which Archbishop Rotherham was the second founder. He had been translated to York from Lincoln, and died of the plague at his palace of Cawood.

(2.) The effigy of Archbishop TOBIAS MATTHEW (died 1628), formerly on his tomb, which is under the second arch from the east, on the south side of the presbytery.

(3.) A monument with a floriated cross, and the bases of pillars, which once supported a canopy. It has been attributed to Archbishop Sewall de Bovil (died 1258), but his tomb, there can be little doubt, remains in the great south transept.

The most easterly bay, between the Lady-chapel and the south aisle, is filled with the tomb and canopy of Archbishop BOWET (1407—1423). Above the elliptical arch of the canopy, the sides of which are panelled, are three very rich tabernacles, with figures. The whole deserves attention, but has been much shattered. "The stone," says Gent, " which covered the grave being thought proper to be removed and sawn for the use of the new pavement, the remains appeared, among which was found nothing remarkable but his archiepiscopal ring, which is gold, and has an odd kind of stone set in it. On the inner verge is engraven, as a Poesy, these words, 'Honneur et Joye.'"[x] Archbishop Bowet had founded the altar of All Saints, at the east end of the south choir aisle. His tomb is on the north side of it.

In the west bay is the high tomb of Archbishop. TOBIAS MATTHEW (1606—1628), with shields in the panels, and a black marble top, restored after the fire. The archbishop, who was famous for his wit and "cheerful sharpness" in discourse, was a special favourite with Elizabeth and James. Between this monument and that of Archbishop Markham is an altartomb, with the effigy, by Noble, of Archbishop MUSGRAVE (1847—1860).

XXI. In the *south* aisle the monuments are :—At the east end, under the window, that of the Hon. THOMAS WATSON WENTWORTH (died 1723), by Guelfi, of Rome. It displays figures of his son and widow. Against the south wall is a grand and stately monument for WILLIAM WENTWORTH, Earl of Strafford (born 1626; died 1695), son of the great Earl, beheaded in 1641. The Earl and his second wife, Henrietta de la Rochefoucauld, stand on either side of an altar. Below is Archbishop LAMPLUGH (1688—1691); an upright figure in a niche, bearing the crosier. (See Pt. II.) Archbishop MATTHEW HUTTON (1747—1757) reclines on his side, in cap, rochet, and black gown. He was the second Matthew Hutton who became Archbishop of York; both were members of the family of Hutton of Marske, near Richmond. The monument of Sir WILLIAM GEE (1611), who is kneeling, with his two wives, is a good example

[x] 'Hist. of York Cathedral,' ii. p. 99.

of its time. Sir William was secretary to James I., and one of his privy council.

On the choir side of the aisle, against one of the arches of the crypt, is the monument of Archbishop DOLBEN (1683—1686); a reclining figure, robed and mitred. (See Pt. II.)

West of the iron grille, which crosses the aisle, are some very striking modern memorial tablets. (1.) For Major OLDFIELD, 5th Bengal Cavalry, Lieutenant-Colonel WILLOUGHBY MOORE, 6th Inniskillings, and those who perished with them in the Europa transport, burnt at sea June 1, 1854. This displays a fine sculpture (part of the scene on board) in high relief, well arranged, and very striking. Executed by Phillip, from a design by G. G. Scott. (2.) A monument to "perpetuate the remembrance of two members of this cathedral church, departed to the mercy of God. William Mason, canon residentiary, and vicar of Aston, whose poetry will be his most endearing monument; and his nephew, William H. Dixon, canon residentiary, and rector of Bishopthorpe (born 1783; died 1854)." The monument, which is much enriched, is of worked brass, with knobs and fruitage of cornelians. On the top of the gable, supported by double shafts, is a figure of the Good Shepherd; at the sides are female figures, one with a cup, the other with a book. Executed by Skidmore, of Coventry, from Scott's design. (3, 4, and 5.) Tablets to the officers and men of the 33rd Regiment who fell during the Russian war, 1854—56; to those of the 84th Regiment (York and Lancaster) who fell during the Indian mutiny; and to those of the 51st who fell in the war with Burmah, 1852, 53. (6.) A very good brass to the officers and men of the 19th Regiment (1st York North Riding) who fell in the Crimean war. At the top is a figure of the Saviour with hands raised in benediction; at the sides are St. Michael, St. George, Gideon, Joshua, Judas Maccabæus, and the Centurion. Executed by Hardman, from Scott's design. The great superiority of these military memorials over most others of their class deserves especial notice.

XXI. The *stained glass* in the choir and its aisles is throughout Perpendicular. Before noticing the windows in detail it will be well to quote Mr. Winston's general observations.

"The earliest Perpendicular glass in the cathedral is contained in the third window from the east in the south aisle of the choir; in the third and fourth windows from the east in the north clerestory of the choir; and in the fourth clerestory window from the east on the opposite side of the choir. These windows are of the close of the fourteenth century. There is also an early Perpendicular Jesse in the third window from the west in the south aisle of the choir. The date of the east window of the choir is well known; a contract for glazing it in three years was made in 1405. This window is one of the best executed that I have ever seen; the beauty of the figures, however, cannot be fully appreciated without inspecting them closely from the gallery near the window. The other windows of the choir aisles, eastward of the small eastern transepts, as well as the glass in the lancet windows on the east side of the great western transepts, appear to be likewise of the time of Henry IV. Some of these windows may probably be a few years earlier than the east window. All the rest of the glass in the choir is of the reigns of Henry V. and Henry VI.; the greater part belonging to the latter reign. The chief peculiarity that I have observed in these windows is, that the white glass, which enters so largely into their composition, is, generally speaking, less green in tint than usual, especially in the western and southern parts of England. Mr. Browne has informed me that it clearly appears, from the Fabric Rolls, that this white glass is of *English* manufacture; which circumstance may perhaps serve to account for its whiteness." [y]

The contract for glazing the great *east window*, between the Dean and Chapter and John Thornton, of Coventry, glazier, is dated December 10, 1405. The original does not exist; but an extract is preserved among the Harleian MSS. Thornton undertakes to " portray the said window with his own hand, and the histories, images, and other things to be painted in it," and to finish it within three years. He is to provide glass, lead, and workmen at the expense of the Chapter; and is to receive, " for every week wherein he shall work in his art," 4*s.*; and each year 5*l.*

[y] 'On the Painted Glass in York.'—In the York vol. of the Archæol. Institute, p. 21.

sterling; and after the work is completed 10*l.* for his reward.[*]

The subjects in the upper division of the window, above the gallery, are from the Old Testament; beginning with the Creation, and ending with the Death of Absalom. All below are from the Book of Revelation, except those in the last or lowest tier, which are representations of kings and bishops. The tracery lights are filled with figures of prophets, kings, and saints, with angels in the uppermost divisions; below a small figure of the Saviour in Judgment, at the apex of the window.

It has already been shown that the tracery of this superb window might have been completed long before 1405, when Thornton commenced his glazing. "The plan pursued in the carrying on of works of this description seems to have been to fill the windows with linen cloth, which gives a sufficient light, or with plain

---

[*] "Indentura inter Dec et Capit Ebor. et Johñ Thornton de Coventre, glasier, sup. vitreacõe magnæ fenestræ in orientali gamolo chori Eccl. Cath. Ebor., qᵈ opus perficiet intra trienniũ ab inchoatione operis, et manu sua propria portroiabit dictam fenestram et historias, imagines, et alia quecunq. pingenda in eisdem, et eãdã depinget quatenus opus fuerit secundũ ordinacõe Decani et Capituli; et præfatus Johẽs etã providebit vitreũ et plũbũ et operarios sumptibus capituli, ad commodũ Decani et Capituli sicut faceret si opus hujusmodi fieri deberet suis sumptibus et expensis, ad qᵈ corporale prestitit juramentum; et dictus Johẽs percipiet a Decano et Capitulo singulis septimanis quibus laborabit in arte sua durante dicto triennio 4s.; et quolibet anno ejusdẽ triennii 5 Lib. sterl., et post opus completũ 10 Lib. pro regardo suo. Dat. Ebor. 10 Dec. 1405. 7. H. 4."

glass, until some benefactor could be found to furnish the glazing, or until it was convenient to employ funds for the purpose." [a]

The stained glass in the *north* aisle, east of the small transept, is of the time of Henry IV. The east window of the aisle has, in the upper part, the Crucifixion, with St. John and the Blessed Virgin, and a figure of St. James below, with other subjects at the sides. The St. James seems to have belonged originally to another window. The magnificent window of the small transept dates probably from the reign of Henry V. (1413—1422). It contains subjects from the life of St. William of York, and representations of miracles attributed to his intercession. The windows westward of this are of somewhat later date. They seem to have been given by —— Thomas Parker, Canon of York, circ. 1423. In the border of this window are repeated the words Thomas Parker, with a hound collared between them. This must have been his badge:—by Robert Wolveden, Treasurer of York, who died in 1432—3, leaving 20*l.* to the fabric. His name is repeated in the borders :—and by Archbishop Bowet (died 1423), whose name and arms occur repeatedly in the glass.

In the *south* aisle the east window is temp. Henry IV. The subjects (from the life of a saint) are not easily interpreted. In the upper part of the central light is the figure of an Apostle, apparently of the same date and character as the figure of St. James in the opposite window. The window adjoining this,

[a] Willis, 'Arch. Hist. of York Cathedral,' p. 44.

south, has been filled with "a very beautiful glass painting, of the last half of the sixteenth century. It was presented to the cathedral by Lord Carlisle in 1804, and was brought from a church at Rouen" (the Church of St. Nicholas). "The design (the Salutation of Mary and Elizabeth) is evidently taken from a painting, I believe by Baroccio (who died in 1612, aged 84), but the colouring and execution have been varied to suit the nature of the material employed. I infer, from the column-like arrangement of the groups, as well as the actual division lines of the glass, that this work was originally painted for a four-light window." [b] The superb colouring of this window deserves especial notice. The third window from the east in this aisle is of earlier date, and contains a fine figure of Edward III. The transept window was probably the gift of the executors of Thomas Longley, Bishop of Durham (died 1437). It displays subjects from the life and miracles of St. Cuthbert, and figures of the principal members of the House of Lancaster. The next window (with a tree of Jesse) is earlier, and no doubt dates from before the end of the fourteenth century. The two remaining windows, one with designs from the life of the Virgin, the other with grand single figures under canopies, are perhaps temp. Henry VI.

In the clerestory windows of the choir, the earlier glass is in the third and fourth from the east, on the north side, and in the fourth from the east, opposite.

[b] C. Winston, 'Stained Glass of York,' p. 22.

This is of the end of the fourteenth century. The rest is later.

XXIII. The *crypt* is entered from the upper part of the choir aisles. Before the fire of 1829, the only crypt that was known to exist, occupied one compartment and a half of the middle aisle, under the platform of the high altar. This was apparently Norman, with some Perpendicular repairs and additions. The repairs consequent on the fire showed that "the pillars and lower parts of the walls of another crypt extended under the whole of the western part of the choir and its side aisles. Also that the crypt above mentioned, which had been so long known, was in fact a mere piece of patchwork, made up during the fitting up of the choir in the fourteenth century, out of the old materials, to support a platform for the altar, and provide chapels and altar room beneath it."[c] This original crypt had been filled up with earth, which was removed, and the whole may now be examined.

The crypt thus laid open is of late Norman character, with massive piers, diapered, and having four small shafts placed round each. Toward the east it opens north and south into a projecting building, "a kind of eastern transept, but which from the greater thickness of its walls was evidently a tower." This crypt was

[c] Willis, 'York Cathedral,' p. 8. Professor Willis's minute description of the crypt is of especial value. There are also long notices of it in Mr. Browne's History; and (with plans and drawings) in a paper by Mr. Robinson in the 'Trans. of Brit. Architects,' vol. i.

no doubt the work of Archbishop Roger (1154—1181) who built the Norman choir which was pulled down when that which now exists was constructed. As at Canterbury, the general design of which cathedral seems to have been closely imitated by Roger, this crypt was entered from its aisles, at the western end of which appears a portion of a vestibule, and of an enriched Norman portal. Adjoining this portal is a low arch, and a portion of an apse; both of earlier date than Roger's work, and belonging to the first Norman cathedral of Archbishop Thomas (1071 — 1100). The apse proves that the transepts of the first Norman church terminated in this form eastward. An arch appears to have carried a spiral turret for a staircase, leading to the upper galleries of the church, such as still exist at Norwich.

The central part of the extreme western portion of this crypt had apparently been filled with earth ever since its first construction by Archbishop Roger. It is enclosed by a massive wall, 3 feet 6 inches in thickness. This is of Roger's time. Within it is a wall, "apparently of great antiquity, 4 feet 8 inches thick; and on the inner side, a third wall, which lines the latter, and is only 2 feet thick. The middle wall is faced with herring-bone work, and of coarse workmanship, and has evidently belonged to one of the early structures, possibly to the Saxon church. . . . . The inner thin wall is partly constructed of old materials, apparently derived from some part of the church that was pulled down to make way for the new crypt."[d] It probably served as a foundation for the timber work of the stalls in the choir above. The middle wall will be regarded with very great interest, if, as is not impossible, it formed part of the stone church built by King Eadwin. (See § 1.) At any rate it marks the exact site of this church, even if we admit that the work of Eadwin was replaced by a more elaborate structure by Archbishop Albert, in the tenth century.

The earth which filled the enclosure made by these walls was removed after 1829. The workmen left however, a slab of stone, about 5 feet higher than the level of the pavement of the crypt, and three steps which they found a little to the east of this slab. These have been regarded as an altar and the ascent to it. But Professor Willis conjectures that "this was the stair which led to the small crypt or 'confession' of the Saxon chancel."[e]

XXIV. The *central tower* of the first Norman cathedral seems to have remained in its original state, at least as high as the roof, after the construction of the Early English transepts. The treasurer, John le Romeyn, who built the north transept, is said also to

[d] Willis, p. 12.

[e] Willis, p. 19. "In the earlier churches, both Saxon and Norman, the crypts were much smaller than in the later ones, and were confined to the extreme east end of the chancel, under the high altar. That of the Saxon chancel at Canterbury was entered in the middle by a stair similar to this."—*Id.* Compare also the remarkable Saxon crypt at Ripon, called St. Wilfrid's Needle.

have built the campanile, or bell-tower.[f] This no doubt refers to the central tower; but Le Romeyn's work was in all probability above the roof. The core of the existing piers is Norman; and Norman ash-laring remains on the north-west pier, in the parts above the vault of the nave aisle.[g] These Norman piers were cased with Decorated or Perpendicular masonry as the works of the nave and choir advanced to them; the western faces of the piers toward the nave first receiving their casing, and the eastern of those toward the choir.[h] After the completion of both nave and choir, the casing of the piers was also completed; and in 1409 Thomas de Haxey was appointed supervisor of the work of the fourth pier; a proof that the three others had already been finished.[i] The lantern or upper part of the tower above the piers, was still in progress in 1421, when a temporary roof was set up,[k] and the stone-work was not completed in 1447.[l] In 1471 the permanent roof was preparing,[m] and was complete in 1472, when the charges for painting it are recorded.[n]

The four great arches of the tower, with their huge piers and capitals of leafage, are magnificent. Above them runs a string-course with projecting angel brackets.

---

[f] Stubbes.   [g] Willis, p. 8.

[h] Willis, p. 39. A most minute and interesting account of the casing of the piers will be found here. The masonry of the piers will be found to be of different levels, showing that the work was taken up at different times on each side of the pier.

[i] See the order in Willis, p. 40.   [k] 'Fabric Rolls,' p. 44.

[l] Id., p. 62.   [m] Id. p. 74.   [n] Id. p. 77.

An enriched wall arcade, with a parapet, intervenes between the main arches and the lofty Perpendicular windows, two in each face. The vault of the lantern, 180 feet from the pavement, is a rich lierne. The effect of the whole, it has been well said, is "beyond all praise."

In the spandrils of the main arches are shields with armorial bearings :—

North side.—3 crowns, 2 and 1—King Edwin.

3 crowns in pale—King Oswald.

West side.—A cross floré between 5 martlets— Edward the Confessor.

Quarterly—Modern France and England.

South side.—6 osiers interlaced in cross—Walter Skirlaw.

2 keys in saltire ; in chief a mitre—Chapter of York.

East side.—3 estoils of 7 points—St. Wilfrid.

A pastoral staff surmounted by a pall charged with 6 cross crosslets fitché—See of York.

In the windows of the lantern are some portions of the original glass, displaying, among other devices, the cross keys of the chapter.

The completion of the central tower terminated the great series of works which had replaced the Norman cathedral by the gigantic building which now exists. The church was accordingly re-consecrated, July 3, 1472.

XXV. A work of no small importance, however, was completed after this date. This was the rood or choir screen; the construction of which may be safely placed between the years 1475 and 1505. William Hyndeley was the master-mason, having two others under him. Six carpenters were employed, and received 11*l*. 16*s*. 4*d*. The sum of 27*s*. 8½*d*. was paid to the sawyers, and 96*s*. and 4*d*. to the labourers, of whom there were but three." ° Among the decorations of the screen occurs Hyndeley's device—a hind lodged, or *lying*.

The screen consists of fifteen compartments, seven on the north, and eight on the south of the central portal. The compartments are divided by buttresses, and in each is a lofty pedestal, supporting a life-sized statue of a king of England, the series ending with Henry VI. Above is a superb mass of tabernacle-work, enriched with small figures; and the screen is finished by a very rich parapet. The portal is in four orders, surmounted by an ogeed pediment. Under the apex of this pediment is a niche, from which the figure is gone; censing angels remain on either side; below are two smaller angels with an organ; and two boys supporting an open book. The figures of angels which fill the lower moulding of the parapet are cast in plaster, and were inserted by Bernasconi. The fine statues of the kings deserve special notice. The original statue of Henry VI. was removed at some unknown period. Like other effigies of the king, at Ripon and elsewhere, it seems to have been regarded with the reverence bestowed on the image of a saint; and it may possibly have been destroyed at the

° 'Fabric Rolls,' p. 8.

G

Reformation. It was afterwards replaced by a figure of James I., which occupied the last niche until very recently. The existing figure of Henry VI. is the work of a local artist.

The screen, rich and beautiful as it is, is perhaps too massive, and certainly does not improve the effect of the transept. Its removal, however, which was threatened during the repairs after the fire of 1829, is entirely to be deprecated.

XXVI. The ancient *Organ* was destroyed in 1829. In 1832 an organ built by Elliot and Hill, from the design of Dr. Camidge, the organist, was presented to the cathedral by the Earl of Scarborough, who was one of the Prebendaries of York. This organ cost 3000*l.* In 1859 it underwent considerable alteration at a cost of more than 1300*l.*, by Messrs. Hill and Son, under the superintendence of the present organist, Dr. Monk. It has now 69 stops and 4266 pipes.

XXVII. On the south side of the choir are the *Record Room*, *Vestry*, and *Treasury*. The Record Room, which is fitted with presses, and contains the valuable series of Registers, Fabric Rolls, and other documents relating to the cathedral, formed part of a chantry founded by Archbishop Zouch about 1350; but rebuilt about the year 1396, so as to bring it into uniformity with the new choir. At its south-west angle is a draw-well, called " St. Peter's Well," " of very wholesome clear water, much drunk by the common people." [p]

[p] Torre.

HORN OF ULPHUS

DETAIL

The vestry and treasury were rebuilt twenty years before Archbishop Zouch's chantry. In the vestry are preserved some antiquities of very great interest: they include the *Horn of Ulphus*, (Plate IX.) made of an elephant's tusk, and dating from a period shortly before the Conquest; when Ulph, the son of Thorald, the lord of great part of eastern Yorkshire, laid this horn on the altar in token that he bestowed certain lands on the church of St. Peter. Among these lands was Godmundham, near Market Weighton, the site of the great pagan temple which was profaned by Coifi, the high priest, after his conversion by St. Paulinus. The horn is encircled about the mouth by a belt of carving, representing griffins, a unicorn, a lion devouring a doe, and dogs wearing collars. The griffins stand on either side of a tree, which at once recalls the conventional sacred tree of Assyrian sculpture; and the whole design has much in common with the patterns on those oriental or Sicilian fabrics largely used for royal robes and priestly vestments long before the Norman Conquest, some of which (See Durham Cathedral, Pt. i., § xxx.) are still preserved in this country, and many in France. This famous horn disappeared during the Civil War; but came into the hands of the Lords Fairfax, one of whom restored it to the church. Its golden ornaments had been removed; but a silver gilt chain and bands were attached to it by the Chapter in 1675.—A magnificent oak chest, carved with the story of St. George, dating early in the fifteenth century.—A silver pastoral staff, 6 feet long, taken, in 1688, from James Smith, titular Bishop of Callipolis, by the Earl of Danby. "The Pope had made Smith his Vicar-apostolic for the northern district, and he was soon pounced upon."[q] The Mazer bowl, or "Indulgence Cup of Archbishop Scrope." This is a bowl of dark-brown wood, with a silver rim, and three silver cherubs' heads, serving as feet. Round the rim is the inscription, "Recharde arche beschope Scrope grantis on to alle tho that drinkis of this cope x dayis to pardune, Robart Gubsune Beschope musm grantis in same forme afore saide x dayis to pardune, Robart Strensalle." The cup seems to have originally been given by Agnes Wyman, wife of Henry Wyman, Mayor of York, to the Corpus Christi Guild. No similar instance of an episcopal consecration of such a cup is known. The Corpus Christi Guild of York was dissolved in 1547; and the cup passed afterwards to the Cordwainers, whose arms appear at the bottom of it. Their association was dissolved in 1808; and the bowl was presented to the Minster by Mr. Hornby, who had become its proprietor. The word "musm" perhaps refers to Richard Messing (Latinized Mesinus), Bishop of Dromore in 1408, and for some time suffragan of York.[r] Three silver chalices with patens, taken from

---

[q] The staff is said to have been wrested from the hand of Bishop Smith, when walking in procession to his 'Cathedral Church.'

[r] There is a short paper on this bowl, by Mr. Davies, of York, in the York vol. of the Archæol. Instit.

the tombs of archbishops. The rings of Archbishops Greenfield, Sewall, and Bowet, from their tombs. An ancient " coronation (installation?) chair" apparently of the fifteenth century.

At the south-east angle of the nave is an apartment called the Record Room.

XXVIII. Passing out of the Minster by the south transept, the exterior of which has already been described, we proceed along the south side of the nave. The bays are separated by lofty buttresses, rising high above the aisle roof. These were originally flying buttresses; but the connexion with the wall of the clerestory has disappeared; how and at what time is uncertain. The buttresses rise above the aisle roof in three stages. In the lowest is a canopied niche containing a figure; and from the second, terminating in three gables, rises the lofty pinnacle of the third. A hollow string-course, decorated with leafage, supports the parapet of the aisle roof, through which the pediment of the windows breaks, and terminates above it in a rich finial of leafage. The base of the parapet is carried round the buttresses; and from it, in front of each buttress, project three gurgoyles—grotesque figures of men and animals. The parapet of the main roof differs in design from that below, and is battlemented.

The enriched buttresses produce the chief effect on this side of the Minster. It may here be said that the fantastic gurgoyles, which are so conspicuous, are more numerous in the later work of York Cathedral than in any other English church of the same rank, and form one of the special characteristics of its exterior.

The central tower, the date of the completion of which has already been given, is well seen from this side. It is 65 feet square, and the largest in England. Winchester, which comes next, being only 62. The gurgoyles projecting from its buttresses,—winged, bat-shaped demons, seem as if expelled from the holy building by the sounds of the choir below.

XXIX. The *West Front* (Frontispiece) admits of being well seen from the end of the open space in front of it. The south side of this space has been happily cleared, of late years, of small buildings, which pressed far too closely on the cathedral.

This famous façade fully deserves its reputation. Other west fronts—such as those of Peterborough, Ely, and Wells, are more picturesque, or have more special interest attached to them. Lincoln has Norman portions which, however interesting and remarkable, prevent us from regarding it as one design. Lichfield may fairly be compared with York, and is perhaps even more graceful; but its details have been ruined, and are now almost entirely of plaster. It may truly be said that the west front of York is more architecturally perfect as a composition and in its details, than that of any other English cathedral. It consists of a centre, flanked by two lofty towers, forming the terminations of the aisles. The towers are divided from the nave by very deep buttresses, which occur again at the exterior angles. The lower part of this front,

including the three portals, and the two lower windows
in the towers, which light the aisles, is of Early Decorated character. All above, as high as the roof, is
later (curvilinear) and is probably of the time of Archbishop Melton (1317—1340). The towers, above the
roof, are Perpendicular. The south-west tower had
been begun in 1433,[s] and was still unfinished in 1447.[t]
It was probably completed before the death, in 1457,
of John Bernyngham, treasurer of York for twenty-
five years, whose name appears on it, and by whose
exertions it was erected.[u] The north-west tower was
not carried on until about 1470.

The central doorway has an outer arch of many
orders, greatly enriched, and subdivided by a central
shaft into two lesser, foliated arches, in the tympanum above which is a circle filled with tracery.
The history of Adam and Eve occurs in the mouldings
of the principal arch, and (in spite of restoration) the
minute foliage of its ornamentation deserves special
notice. A crocketed pediment rises above the sill of the
great west window : and the space between the portal
and the buttresses has a double series of enriched
niches. In a niche within the pediment is the figure
of an archbishop, either that of John le Romeyn, who
commenced the nave, or of William of Melton, under
whom the west front was completed. On either side, in
niches beyond the pediment, are the mailed figures of
Percy and Vavasour, the traditional donors of the wood
and stone for the Minster, with their shields of arms

---

[s] 'Fabric Rolls,' p. 51.   [t] Id. p. 62.   [u] Id. p. 68.

adjoining. One of these figures bears a block of wrought stone—the other, what may be either an unwrought stone or a block of timber.[x] Over the portal is the great west window, with an enriched pediment above it, rising into the gable. The gable itself is battlemented, and is crowned with a rich finial.

The buttresses are much enriched with niches and panelling. Figures of saints remain in the upper niches; and in the two lowest, north and south, is some sculpture which has so nearly perished, that the subjects are not easily deciperable. That of one appears to be the Flight into Egypt. The great depth of these buttresses is especially striking.

The towers are 201 feet from the ground. Their windows, above the roof, are completely Perpendicular. Each tower is crowned by a rich battlement, with pinnacles. The fire of 1840 greatly injured the southwest tower, in which it commenced; and some of the delicate stone-work of the exterior has been renewed in consequence. The bells in this tower were destroyed. A new peal, twelve in number, was placed in it in 1843, when Dr. Beckwith bequeathed 2000l.

[x] These figures have been re-worked by Michael Taylor, of York. The tradition that the Percys gave much of the wood for the building, is confirmed by many entries in the 'Fabric Rolls.' Stone, from the quarry at Thevesdale, had been granted to the Minster about the beginning of the 13th century, by William de Percy; and about the year 1225, a Charter of Robert le Vavasour occurs, granting free right of way to this quarry. This Charter is printed in Raine's 'Fabric Rolls,' p. 147.

PLATE X.

YORK CATHEDRAL.

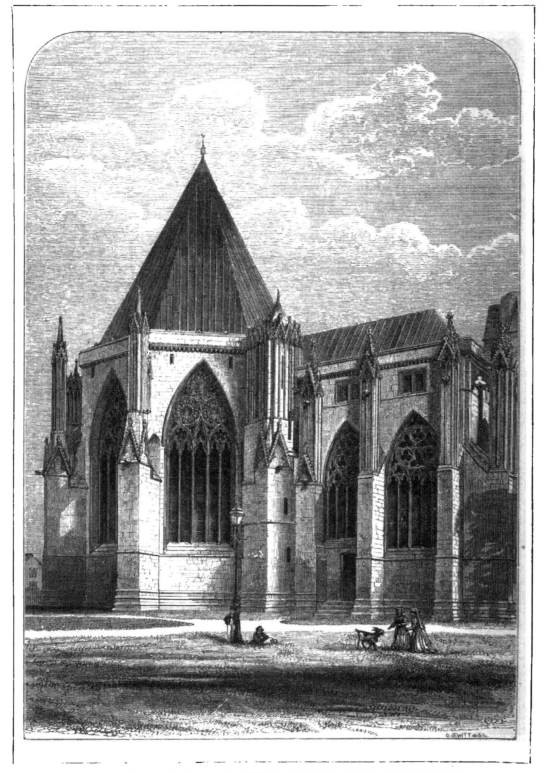

YORK CATHEDRAL. CHAPTER HOUSE AND VESTIBULE.

for this purpose. A monster bell, the largest at present in England, was hung in the north-west tower in 1845. Its height is 7 feet 2 inches, its diameter 8 feet 4 inches, and its weight 10 tons 15 cwt. It was cast by Messrs. Mears, of London, at a cost of 2000*l.*, raised by the inhabitants of York. Like other great bells, it is not rung, but struck with a hammer.

XXX. The north side of the nave is far less enriched than the south; and the plain buttresses do not rise above the parapet of the aisle. This side was concealed by the archbishop's palace. Towards the west end was the chapel of the Holy Sepulchre, founded by Archbishop Roger.

The exterior of the north transept should be especially noticed. Its north front is one of the most remarkable features of the Minster; and has been pronounced, with some justice, "the most noble Early English composition in the kingdom." An arcade covers the wall below the "five sisters"; and on either side of the five lancets above, is a blind arch, filling up the gable. The vestibule of the Chapter-house covers the east transept aisle, and thereby deprives the composition of its proper balance; but the grand simple lines of the front call for the highest admiration.

The Chapter-house, with its vestibule (Plate X.), projects beyond the transept. Each bay of the former is divided by a short flying buttress which deserves attention. It is solid to the height of 49 feet; then has an

arch of a flying buttress, and is again joined towards
the top by a flat panelling. The buttress terminates
above the wall in a spire, with finial of leafage. All
these details, and the windows, are of early Decorated
character. But among the many grotesque gurgoyles
which project from the buttresses and from the vestibule, occur several bears, which have been regarded
as the device of Francis Fitzurse, who became treasurer
of the Minster in 1335. If this supposition be correct,
it must have been some time after this date that the
Chapter-house was completed.

The view east of the Chapter-house is a very fine
one. The choir with its short transept, the central
tower, and the Chapter-house, full of varied lines and
intersections, produces a most picturesque and striking
group. The four bays east of the small transept belong to the earlier period (1361—1373); the transept
itself and the four western bays, to the later (1380—
1405). The most marked difference between these
portions is in the arrangement of the triforium passage,
which, in the presbytery (east of the transepts), is outside instead of, as usual, inside the building. The
passage is between the clerestory windows and a remarkable open screen, " in composition a square-headed
window of three lights, cinque-foiled in the head, and
once transomed." (See Plate I., *ante,*—the south side
of the choir—in which this outer passage is shown).
The lofty transept window should also be noticed.
Many gurgoyles—apes, dragons, and bat-like demons—
project from the main buttresses. The buttresses at

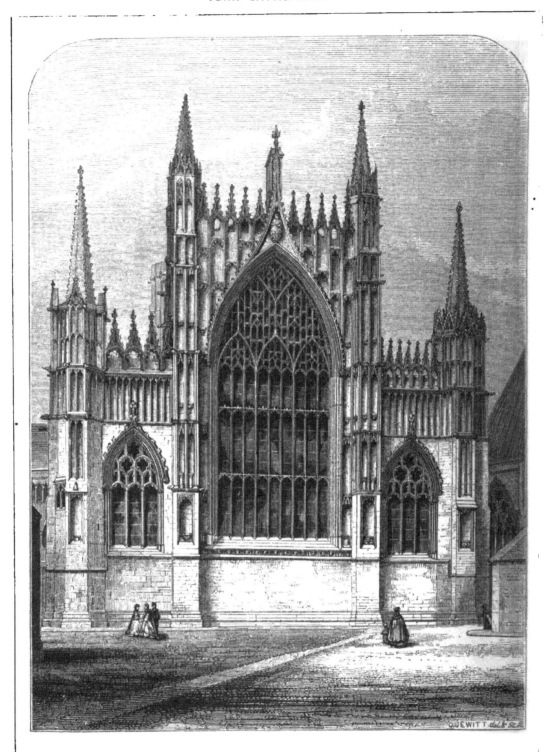

YORK CATHEDRAL. EAST END.

the sides of the transept terminate in straight shafts pierced by projecting gurgoyles; the straight line repeating the character of the outer screen of the clerestory.

XXXI. The east end of the choir (Plate XI.) is only second as a composition, to the west front. The great eastern window forms the centre, crowned by an ogeed drip-stone, rising into a lofty finial far above the parapet. Between the drip-stone and the apex of the window is the figure of an archbishop, probably Thoresby, under whom the presbytery was completed. The massive buttresses on either side are enriched with niches and panel-work, and rise into lofty pinnacles of great beauty. The panelling is continued along the space between the window and the buttresses; and rises above the roof so as to form an open parapet; much enriched. The buttresses which flank the aisles are also capped with lofty pinnacles. The parapets of the aisles differ: that of the south aisle being inferior to the north. This is a restoration. In the lowest niches of the aisle buttresses were not long since figures of the Percy and the Vavasour; with their shields. Under the sill of the great window is a row of seventeen sculptured busts, representing the Saviour with his Apostles; a crowned head (Edward III.) at the north; and a bishop (Thoresby) at the south end.

The best point for examining the east front is about halfway down the opening before it, near the gateway of St. William's College.

The south side of the choir (see Plate I. *ante*) resembles that north. The two parapets however, with the finials of the aisle windows, were not added until 1473, when they were supplied chiefly by the liberality of the Dean, Richard Andrew.[y]

XXXII. Archbishop Roger (1154—1181), besides rebuilding the choir of his cathedral, erected the archiepiscopal palace on the north side, of which the only remaining portions are—the fragment of a *cloister* on the north side of the precincts, in which a wide circular arch encloses two smaller, with trefoil headings; and the building now used as the Chapter-library, but originally, in all probability, the chapel of the archbishop's palace. At the west end are five lancets under a circular arch, showing the transitional character of Roger's work.

The library contains about 8000 vols.; some of which are of great rarity and interest. Among the *MSS.* are —two York Breviaries; 'Tractatus Varii Patrum,' with Ailred of Rievaulx 'de bello Standardi' at the end. The book, which is of the thirteenth century, belonged to Rievaulx; 'Speculum Spiritualium'—from the Carthusian Priory of Mount Grace, near Arncliffe; the Sentences of Peter Lombard (fourteenth century), from St. Mary's of York; Book of Psalms, with Glossary (thirteenth century); some Bibles, one of great beauty,

[y] "Diversis cementarîs facientibus ij batelmentes unum superius et aliud inferius, cum finyall, ex parte australi chori eccl. Cath. Ebor., ultra c marcas per venerabilem virum, magistrum Ricardum Andrew, Decanum Eccl. Ebor., ad idem opus ex sua devocione concessas et collatas 24*l*. 13*s*. 5*d*."—*Fabric Rolls*, p. 80.

temp. Edward I., with small miniatured capitals; MSS. of Cicero (eleventh and twelfth centuries); and a MS. volume by Gray, the poet, containing poems and notes on the history of English poetry, &c. Among the *printed books* are many Caxtons, Wynkyn de Wordes, and Pynsons.

Corbel (York).

YORK CATHEDRAL.

PART II.

History of the See, with Short Notices of the principal Archbishops.[a]

IT is certain that Christianity had been introduced, and had, perhaps, spread extensively, in the north of Britain during the Roman period. Three British bishops, among them a bishop of Eburacum, were present at the Council of Arles in A.D. 314; and tradition (in this case not very trustworthy) has handed down the names of many bishops of York before Paulinus. It is with Paulinus, however, that the real succession of the Northumbrian prelates commences.

Gregory the Great, in sending Paulinus and his companions to St. Augustine in England, desired that a metropolitan might be established at York, with twelve suffragans beneath him; in the same manner as Canterbury. This was never fully accomplished. Paulinus received the pall as metropolitan or archbishop; but none of his successors

[a] The lives of the Archbishops of York have been written by the Rev. W. H. Dixon and the Rev. James Raine, both Canons of York. The first volume (London, 1863), ranging from the foundation of the see to the death of Archbishop Thoresby (1373), is entirely by Canon Raine. Very great use has been made of it in the following notices. The second volume is not yet (1868) published.

were so invested until the accession of Egbert in 732, who went to Rome for that express purpose. The prelates who sat at York between Paulinus and Egbert were known only as "bishops of York," or "of the Northumbrians." The later bishops who received the pall were at first archbishops of the Northumbrians, and afterwards of York. The great diocese was divided by Theodore, Archbishop of Canterbury in 678 (see post, WILFRID). Besides York, the sees of Lindisfarne, Hexham, and Whitherne were then established.

The northern province now embraces the dioceses of York, Durham, Carlisle, Chester, Ripon, Manchester, and Sodor and Man. The sees of Lindisfarne and Hexham became merged in that of Durham. That of Carlisle was established by Henry I. Chester was assigned to the province of York on its erection into an episcopal see by Henry VIII. The sees of Ripon and Manchester were created in 1836 and 1848. Until the 13th century the Bishop of Sodor and Man was a suffragan under the see of Drontheim in Norway. The Scottish bishops were, nominally at least, suffragans of York until Sixtus IV., at the end of the 15th century, assigned the Scottish primacy to the Archbishop of St. Andrews.

Between Canterbury and York there were incessant disputes for supremacy, or at least for equality, until, at a great synod held in 1072, the northern province was formally subjected to the southern. This decision was reversed by the Pope, Honorius II. (1125), and the two metropolitans have thenceforth been independent of each other. But the struggle for precedency continued long afterwards; and in order to settle it the Pope (1354) conferred on the two prelates the titles they still bear—Primate of England (York), and Primate of All England (Canterbury).

[A.D. 627—633.] PAULINUS, the first Christian missionary to the kingdom of Northumbria, left Italy in 601, at the bidding of Gregory the Great, to assist St. Augustine in his work of conversion. With Paulinus came Mellitus, Justus, and Rufinianus; and they brought to Augustine a letter from Gregory, in which the Pope expressed a desire that York should become a metropolitical see, with twelve suffragans. For many years Paulinus assisted Augustine and Justus in the south of England; and in 625, when Eadwin of Northumbria, still a pagan, married the Christian Æthelburh, daughter of Æthelberht of Kent, who had received St. Augustine, Paulinus went with her to her husband's kingdom, having been consecrated by Archbishop Justus (July 21, 625) Bishop of the Northumbrians. The story of his labours in the north, and the manner in which he succeeded in effecting the conversion of Eadwin and of his principal chiefs will be found in every ecclesiastical history, and need not be detailed here. The famous conference between Paulinus and the Northumbrian thegns, at which Christianity—"doctrina eatenus inaudita," as, according to Bede, it was described by Eadwin—was first generally accepted, took place, in all probability, at a royal villa on the site of the present Londesborough, in the East Riding, which, of Roman foundation, had been adopted by the first Northumbrian kings. The great pagan temple, profaned by the high priest Coifi and then destroyed, was certainly at Godmundham, near Market Weighton, and a very short distance from Londesborough. The present church of Godmundham possibly occupies the site of the temple. Shortly after this conference the baptism of Eadwin took place at York on Easter Day (April 12), 627. Two of his children, and many other persons of noble birth, were baptised at the same time. Round the baptistery, which had been hastily built, the king caused a small stone church to be constructed, which became the nucleus of the present cathedral. (See Part I. §§ I., XXIII.)

The kingdom of Eadwin embraced the whole country from the Humber to the Clyde and the Forth, and there are traces of Paulinus and his labours in many parts of this vast district. According to Bede, he used to baptise in the river Swale, near "Cataractum"—the modern Catterick. Local tradition asserts that he baptised at Brafferton, also on the Swale; and the position of the church on the brink of the river may have been intended to commemorate the fact. "Paulin's Carr" and the "Cross of Paulinus," in the adjoining parish of Easingwold, are both mentioned in an Inquisition of the reign of Edward I. Ancient crosses with which his name was connected existed at Dewsbury and at Whalley; and "Paulin's Well" and "Pallinsburn" occur in Northumberland; where also, at "Adgebrin," or Yeavering, near the Cheviots, he is said to have spent thirty-six days in catechising the converts and baptising them in the river Glen. Eadwin's kingdom—or at least his influence—extended at one time south of the Humber. In the ancient Lindsey, at the instance of Blecca, the "prefect" of Lincoln, whom he had converted, Paulinus built a church on or near the site afterwards crowned by the great cathedral of Lincoln, and he is said to have founded the church of Southwell.

In 633 Eadwin fell in the battle of Haethfeld or Hatfield Chase. It was unsafe for the Queen to remain in Northumbria, and Paulinus returned with her to Kent, where he presided over the see of Rochester until his death in 644. He was buried in the chapter-house of the cathedral there, but Archbishop Lanfranc translated his relics and placed them in a silver shrine. The name of Paulinus was inserted in the Calendar, and he became the great patron saint of Rochester.

It is remarkable that Nennius asserts that the person who baptised Eadwin and the converts of Northumbria was named Rum, the son of Urien; and suggestions have accordingly been made that on the death of Urien of Reged his son Rum retired to Rome, became a monk and a priest, and was afterwards sent to England under the name of

Paulinus. But the picture of Paulinus which Bede received from the Abbot of "Peartaneu," in Lincolnshire, to whom it had been given by an old man whom Paulinus, in presence of Eadwin, had baptised in the Trent, seems to be that of a true Italian. "Vir longæ staturæ, paululum incurvus, nigro capillo, facie macilenta, naso adunco pertenui, venerabilis simul et terribilis aspectu."

[A.D. 633—664.] Paulinus had been "Archbishop of the Northumbrians" (he had received the pall after Eadwin's conversion from the Pope Honorius [b]), and his labours extended throughout Eadwin's kingdom. After his departure, Deira, the southern portion of Yorkshire, seems to have been long without a Christian teacher, and to have relapsed for the most part into paganism. Oswald of Northumbria, who had taken refuge with the King of Scotland, embraced Christianity during his exile; and on his succession to the throne of Northumbria applied to Donald of Scotland for a teacher who should aid in converting his people. Corman, a monk of Iona, was first sent, and failed. AIDAN (635—651), also a monk of Iona, succeeded. He fixed the place of his see at Lindisfarne, and had three successors: FINAN (651—661); COLMAN 661—resig. 664); and TUDA (664—5), who are rather to be regarded as bishops of Bernicia (the northern province of Northumberland) than as bishops of the "Northumbrians:" not only because none of them received the pall and their rule extended little into Deira, but because it was the see of Lindisfarne, from which the great bishopric of Durham was in due course developed (see *Durham Cathedral*, Part II.). These bishops all recognised the teaching and followed the observances of the Scottish Church. In the year 664 occurred the Council at Streonshal (Whitby), in which the Scottish party was defeated, and judgment as to the observance of Easter and the other

[b] Beda, H. E., L. ii. c. 16.

questions in debate was given in favour of Rome. Colman then resigned his see; and Tuda, his successor, was, together with nearly all his monks, swept away by a pestilence in the year of his consecration.

[A.D. 664—669.] Through the influence of Alchfrid, ruling in Deira under his father Oswi, King of Northumbria, the famous WILFRID was induced to accept the northern bishopric, and refusing to be consecrated by the British bishops went into Gaul for that purpose. During his absence, which continued for three years, Oswi was gained by the Scottish party, who persuaded him to appoint Ceadda (St. Chad) to the vacant see, which he fixed at York. Ceadda still recognised the Scottish teaching. He was consecrated by Wina, Bishop of Winchester, and two British bishops. Wilfrid, on his return, found no place for himself at York, and retired to his old monastery at Ripon. In 669, Theodore, Archbishop of Canterbury, came to England, and speedily visited the northern province, which was still without a metropolitan, Ceadda being only Bishop of York. He found fault with Ceadda's election and consecration, and the latter voluntarily resigned his bishopric in favour of Wilfrid. Ceadda retired to Lastingham, his former monastery, and was shortly afterwards appointed by Theodore to the vacant see of Mercia (see *Lichfield Cathedral*, Part II.).

[A.D. 669—abandoned 678.] WILFRID, the great champion of the Roman party, took possession of the see of York on Ceadda's resignation. As Bishop of York, Wilfrid restored the minster which Eadwin and Oswald had erected (Part I. § I.), and built much throughout his vast diocese, most noticeably the great minsters at Hexham and at Ripon. Wilfrid was out of favour with Ecgfrid of Northumbria and his Queen, when Theodore of Canterbury came into the north of England in 678, and, without consulting Wilfrid, divided the great Northumbrian diocese, over the whole of which he had ruled, into four

bishoprics—placing the sees at York, Lindisfarne, Hexham,
and Whitherne. Wilfrid rebelled against this "plunder,"
and went to Rome with an appeal to the Pope. He returned
about 680 with the papal decision in his favour, but found
it little regarded in Northumbria. Wilfrid was imprisoned
and at last banished. In 686, at the intercession of Archbishop Theodore, he was reconciled to Alchfrid, then King
of Northumbria. The vacant sees of Lindisfarne and Hexham were given to Wilfrid, but he left them soon afterwards for York, which had been held since 678 by Bosa,
who seems now to have retired. Within two or three
years afterwards Wilfrid again quarrelled with the King,
and left Northumbria. Bosa was replaced in the see of
York, which Wilfrid never recovered, though he returned
at a later period to Northumbria.

[A.D. 678—705.] Bosa, the first Bishop of York, or Deira,
after the division of the great Northumbrian diocese, had
been educated at Whitby under the Abbess Hilda. Little
is known of him. "It is probable that he lost his position
on Wilfrid's return in 686 or 687; but he regained it in
the course of two or three years and held it until his death,
which occurred in 705."[b] His successor

[A.D. 705—718.] John, better known as St. John of
Beverley, was also one of St. Hilda's pupils: "a circumstance," says Fuller, "which soundeth something to her
honour and nothing to his disgrace, seeing eloquent Apollos
himself learned the primar of his Christianity partly from
Priscilla."

St. John, whose foundation at Beverley became one of
the three centres of Christianity in Deira (the others were
York and Ripon), was born of noble parents at Harpham,
in the East Riding. At an early age he began to preach
to the still half-heathen people, arresting their attention by
his powerful eloquence. The Venerable Bede was one of

[b] Raine.

St. John's pupils, and was ordained by him. In 687, John, who had for some time been living in a hermitage at Harneshalg, or Harneshow, on the left bank of the Tyne, opposite Hexham, was consecrated Bishop of Hexham—the see which had been established in 681. Here he remained for eighteen years, during which we know little of his labours or his life. He was translated to York in 705, where he became a favourite with King Osred, and was present at a synod in which many enactments were made for the better regulation of the Northumbrian Church. He was most diligent in watching over his monasteries, and in attending to the poor, and to the company of pupils always gathered about him. Whilst holding the see of York John became the owner of Inderawood, a village on the site of the present Beverley, and in his native district. There was already at Inderawood a small church, dedicated to St. John the Evangelist. This the bishop enlarged, and established a monastery for both sexes (as was then usual) in connection with it. Numerous gifts were made to the new foundation, and many churches were built in the surrounding district, then thickly covered with forest. St. John resigned the see of York in 718, and retired to his monastery at Beverley, where he died in 721. He was canonised, in 1037, by Benedict IX., and in the same year his relics were translated by Archbishop Alfric and deposited in a shrine of gold. At the Reformation they were interred in a case of lead, which has been twice exposed to the light—in 1664 and in 1736.

The reputation of St. John of Beverley was greater than that of any northern saint, St. Cuthbert of Durham being alone excepted. Athelstane, on his way into Scotland in A.D. 934, visited the shrine, and carried off the holy banner of the saint as a protection to his host, promising that if he returned victorious he would bestow many privileges on the church. He did so accordingly, giving to it its famous right of sanctuary, and founding a college of secular canons. The traditional words in which the grant of sanctuary is recorded—

> " Als fre make I the
> As hert may thenk
> Or eghe may see,"

are certainly very ancient, and are mentioned in a confirmation of the privileges of the church made by Henry IV.

The Conqueror and Stephen were prevented by miraculous interference, as it was alleged, from ravaging the territory of St. John. The banner of Beverley was one of those which floated over the host of the English at the Battle of the Standard (1138, see *post, Archbishop Thurstan*); and Edward I., like Athelstane, carried it with him into Scotland. Henry V. and his Queen visited the shrine of St. John after the victory of Agincourt, Oct. 25, the festival of his translation; and although St. Crispin and Crispinian shared the honours of the day, the King attributed the victory greatly to the intercession of St. John of Beverley.

[A.D. 718—732.] *WILFRID II., in whose favour St. John resigned the see of York, had been one of his pupils. Little is known of him. He resigned the see in 732, devoting the last portion of his life to solitude and prayer: in what place is uncertain. He died in 744 or 745.

[A.D. 732—766.] EGBERT, cousin of Ceolwulf, King of Northumbria, to whom Bede dedicates his history, succeeded Wilfrid. "His first endeavour was to obtain the pall, which was given to him by Gregory III. at Rome, in 735. He thus became the second Archbishop of York. More than a century had elapsed since Paulinus fled into Kent, carrying his pall with him, and no one since that time had sought for the lost honour: a neglect which was made, in after years, a strong argument for the precedence of Canterbury, when the famous controversy arose between the two metropolitan sees. When Egbert thus became archbishop he stepped at once into a commanding position, and every bishop in the northern province was made his suffragan.[c] Egbert was a stern disciplinarian, and it was soon after his consecration to the see that Bede addressed to him his well-known letter, setting forth the disorder and corruption of the whole northern diocese, — evils which throughout his episcopate Egbert sought by every means to reform. He was probably the first introducer of the parochial system in the north, and was certainly the founder of the famous monastic school of York and of the library connected with it. In this school Alcuin was educated, and afterwards became " magister scholarum." His poems contain many references to the piety, energy, and goodness of his old master.

The Pontifical of Egbert has been published by the Surtees Society. His 'Excerptiones'—extracts from the Fathers and from the Canons on matters of discipline; a dialogue; 'De Ecclesiastica Institutione;' a Confessional, and a Penitential; will all be found in Thorpe's 'Ancient Laws and Institutes of England.' Eadbert, the brother of Egbert, became King of Northumbria in 738. In 757 he resigned the crown, and entered his brother's so-called "monasterium" at York. Both King and Archbishop were buried in one of the porches (porticus) or chapels in the cathedral.

[A.D. 766—782.] ALBERT, the son of powerful and wealthy parents, had been "Vice-dominus," or "Abbas," of Egbert's monastic school. The reputation of that school, which had spread all over Europe, was due quite as much to the zeal and learning of Albert as to the energy of his predecessor in the see of York; and the great library was chiefly collected by the former during many wanderings on the Continent, with Alcuin for his companion.

[c] Raine i. p. 95. "Cæteri episcopi inter Paulinum et Egbertum nichil altius quam simplicis episcopi vocabulo anhelarunt."— Anglia Sacra, i. 66.

As Archbishop, Albert did much for the minster, almost rebuilding it after it had been greatly injured by fire (see Part I., § I.). Two years before his death he retired from the care of his province, having consecrated Eanbald as his coadjutor. He died in his cell in the "monasterium" attached to the cathedral, November, 782.

[A.D. 782—796.] EANBALD was destined to witness the first fierce attacks of the heathen Danes on Northumbria. The country was so widely ravaged, and was in such entire disorder, that in 790 Alcuin deserted York for the Court of Charles the Great. Eanbald died at the monastery of Etlete or Edete—the site of which is unknown.

[A.D. 796—812.] EANBALD II., a favourite pupil of Alcuin, succeeded. Alcuin himself would no doubt have been elected, had he chosen to return to Northumbria; and he wrote frequently to the new archbishop, laying down many rules for the direction of his province. Alcuin sent to York, among other gifts, a ship's load of metal (stagnum) for the roofing of the minster bell tower.[d]

Of five succeeding archbishops—

[A.D. 812—831.] WULFSY.

[A.D. circ. 837—854?] WIGMUND.

[A.D. 854—890?] WULFERE.

[A.D. circ. 895.] ETHELBALD, and

[A.D. circ. 928.] REDEWALD.

little or nothing is known. At this period the history of Northumbria is very obscure, and the whole country was ravaged by the Northmen. York was taken by them in the year 867.

[A.D. 928—956.] WULSTAN is said to have been raised to the see by Athelstane, who first incorporated Northumbria with the "Empire" of Britain. After Athelstane's death, however, Wulstan joined the Danish party, and in 947 assisted in making Eric, son of Harold Harfagre, King of Northum-

[d] Ut Domuscula cloccarum stagno tegatur. Alc. Op. i. 231.

bria. Edred, in 952, seized the archbishop, and imprisoned him at Jedburgh. The King afterwards allowed him to resume his episcopal functions at Dorchester; but Wulstan died in 955 at Oundle, in Northamptonshire, and was there interred.

[A.D. 956—972.] OSKYTEL, whose Danish name indicates the extent of northern influence and settlement, was a friend and coadjutor of St. Dunstan. In 950 he had been made Bishop of Dorchester; and was translated to York in 956. Little is known of him. A certain ETHELWOLD is said by two chroniclers (Symeon of Durham and Stubbes) to have succeeded; but if this was the case he can have held the see but a short time; since

[A.D. 972—992) in the year of Oskytel's death OSWALD became Archbishop of York; holding the see together with that of Worcester, to which he had been raised in 961. Oswald was the son of noble Danish parents. Odo, Archbishop of Canterbury, was his uncle; and he was related to Oskytel, his predecessor in the see of York. He was sent by Archbishop Odo to Winchester, where the lives of the secular canons by no means satisfied him; and he accordingly transferred himself to the famous Benedictine Monastery of Fleury, where he took the vows, and was afterwards ordained. On the death of Odo he returned to England, and was warmly received by Archbishop Oskytel, who had just become the head of the Northern Province. Oswald set out with Oskytel for Rome; but did not proceed beyond Fleury, where he remained until Oskytel summoned him again to England to assist in the re-introduction of the Benedictine rule, and the suppression of the secular canons. He joined cordially in the endeavours of Dunstan to this effect, and was raised by his influence to the see of Worcester in 961. In 972 he became Archbishop of York; but retained Worcester in commendam until his death.

Oswald was the reformer and remodeller of many religious

houses in his diocese of Worcester, and was powerful enough to rearrange the great monasteries of Ely and St. Albans. In the north he does not appear to have made, or perhaps to have been able to make, much change. He died and was buried at Worcester; where his shrine was held in great honour, and where St. Oswald and St. Wulstan were regarded as the patrons of the see. The most important life of St. Oswald is by an unknown monk of Ramsey—a monastery founded at his instance by Æthelwine, Ealdorman of East Anglia, called by the chroniclers "Amicus Dei." This life remains in MS. in the British Museum (Nero, E. 1), and is the foundation on which all subsequent biographers of the archbishop have built.

[A.D. 992—1002.] ADULF, Abbot of Peterborough, succeeded to the sees of both York and Worcester, and held both till his death. Little is recorded of him.

[A D. 1002—1023.] WULSTAN II., like his two predecessors, was bishop at once of York and of Worcester. It was probably intended that the sees should continue united; and the arrangement was confirmed by Edward the Confessor, on the ground that, Northumbria being ravaged by the Danes, the possession of the southern bishopric was necessary for the maintenance of the northern primate.[e] However this may be, LEOFSI was appointed bishop of Worcester in 1016, probably as suffragan to Wulstan.

Wulstan is believed to have been the author of certain homilies to which the name of "Lupus Episcopus" is prefixed, and which remain in MS. with the exception of one —an address on the Danish invasion. He died at York, but was buried by his special desire in the monastic church at Ely.

[A.D. 1023—1050.] ALFRIC PULTA became Archbishop of York only, Leofsi being succeeded at Worcester by Living, the great counsellor of Cnut. When Living was accused

[e] Thomas's 'Worcester,' Appendix I., referred to by Raine, p. 132.

of being implicated in the murder of Alfred, the archbishop
seized on the see of Worcester, which he resigned, however,
in the following year, and permitted Living (who was
Bishop of Crediton as well as of Worcester) to return.
Alfric died at Southwell, and was buried at Peterborough.

[A.D. 1050—1060.] KINSI, a monk of Peterborough, succeeded.
Like Alfric he was buried in the church of that famous
monastery.

[A.D. 1060—1069.] EALDRED, the successor of Kinsi, was a
person of extraordinary influence and energy. He had been
brought up in the monastery of Winchester, and was
appointed Abbot of Tavistock, no doubt by the influence of
Living, Bishop of Crediton and Worcester. In 1046
Bishop Living died, and was buried at Tavistock. Leofric
succeeded him in the see of Crediton, and Ealdred the
Abbot in that of Worcester.

Ealdred was in great favour with the Confessor, and in
1049 he went with Herman, Bishop of Sherburn, to Rome,
where they induced the Pope to absolve their master from
the vow he had made of going on pilgrimage to that city.
In 1054 Ealdred was sent on an embassy to the Emperor
Henry III., at Cologne, where he remained a whole year,
and prevailed on the Emperor to allow his nephew, the son
of Edmund Ironside, to return to England. In 1058
Ealdred made a pilgrimage to Jerusalem,—the first English
bishop who had done so. More than once he was the
leader of expeditionary forces against the princes of Wales.
From 1055 to 1058 he had charge of the see of Sherburn,
which Herman had resigned, but which he resumed in the
latter year. In 1056 the Bishop of Hereford was killed
during a Welsh foray. The see was committed in commendam to Ealdred, who held it until his translation to
York in 1060. He then resigned Hereford, but retained
Worcester.

On his accession to York, Ealdred went to Rome to
receive the pall, accompanied by Tosti, Earl of Northumbria,

the brother of Harold. The Pope refused to confer it, being indignant at the proposed tenure of two sees by one person, and that his license had not been demanded for Ealdred's promotion. He deprived the bishop of all his honours; and Ealdred quitted Rome in disgrace. But after he had gone a day's journey from the city, he and his company were attacked by thieves, who stripped them of everything. He returned to Rome, and made a last appeal to the mercy of the Pope. It was successful. Ealdred promised to resign the see of Worcester, which he did on his return, and consecrated Wulstan as his successor.

As Archbishop, Ealdred built and endowed much throughout his province, establishing stalls at Southwell, and doing much for Beverley. In 1066 he crowned Harold; and after Hastings, met the Conqueror at Berkhampstead, and took the oaths of allegiance. On "Midwinter day" in the same year (1066) he crowned William in the Abbey Church of Westminster, Stigand of Canterbury not being allowed to officiate. He also consecrated Matilda queen in 1068. Ealdred was a fearless champion of the rights of the church; and the troubles which fell upon the north after the Conquest are said to have affected him so greatly that he died of a broken heart, Sept. 11, 1069. He was buried in the Minster—not more than a few months before the church and its surrounding buildings were destroyed by fire, during the attack on York by the sons of Sweyn and the Northmen.

[A.D. 1070—1100.] THOMAS OF BAYEUX was the first Norman Archbishop of York. His father was a priest; and Thomas, with his brother Sampson, who afterward became Bishop of Worcester, were taken under the protection of Odo, Bishop of Bayeux, by whom they were sent to study at Liege and elsewhere. Thomas accompanied Odo to England, where he was made one of the King's chaplains, and was raised in 1070 to the see of York. He was appointed at Easter, but could not be consecrated until after Lanfranc, in August of the same year, became Archbishop of Canterbury. Thomas made a vain attempt to preserve the independence of his see, but was compelled to promise subjection to Lanfranc himself, though not to his successors. In 1071 both archbishops went to Rome to receive their palls, accompanied by Remigius, Bishop of Dorchester. (He afterwards removed the place of the see to Lincoln). At Rome, and afterwards in England, the controversy between York and Canterbury was duly considered, and at a synod held in the presence of the Conqueror, it was settled that the Humber should be the southern boundary of the province of York, and that the northern archbishops should swear allegiance to Canterbury, and should be consecrated in Canterbury Cathedral. Worcester also, which for a short time had been subjected to York, was for the future subordinated to Canterbury.

Archbishop Thomas was present in 1075 at the Council of London; and at the funeral of Lanfranc at Canterbury in 1089. He officiated occasionally in the southern province during the vacancy (1089—1093) between the death of Lanfranc and the appointment of Anselm, and consecrated the latter prelate; first insisting that the words "Primate of all England," inserted in Anselm's petition for consecration should be removed. (The words "Metropolitan of Canterbury" were accordingly substituted.) Although Malmesbury and some other chroniclers assert that Thomas crowned Henry I., the real facts, as recorded by Hugh the Chantor, were that Henry, fearing delay, caused himself to be crowned by certain of the southern bishops before Thomas could reach him. The Archbishop paid his homage and returned at once to York, where he died in November of the same year, 1100.

Archbishop Thomas had found his diocese suffering from the devastation inflicted on it by the Conqueror. Much of the city of York, including the minster, with its famous library, had been destroyed by fire; and every monastery in the north had perished. Thomas rebuilt his cathedral (Pt. I. § i.), and remodelled its constitution. The number of canons had hitherto been seven. They were now increased, and instead of an " Abbas," as their superior had been called, a dean was appointed. The Archbishop supported and assisted the restoration of Whitby Abbey and St. Mary's at York; Benedictine houses, which had become ruinous and deserted.[f] He was buried in his own cathedral. Malmesbury describes him as of noble presence, of great excellence of life, and possessed of very unusual learning. He was an excellent musician, and the verses on the tomb of the Conqueror were composed by him.

[A.D. 1101—1108.] GERARD, translated from Hereford, was the nephew of Walkeline, Bishop of Winchester, and therefore a connexion of the Conqueror. In the long disputes between Anselm and Henry I., Gerard took the side of the King, and it was perhaps for this reason, among others, that he was no favourite with the chroniclers. He is said to have been " deceitful and of evil life;" and when he died in the garden of his palace at Southwell, on his way to London, his sudden death was recorded as a judgment. The Canons would not inter his corpse within the minster, though it was afterwards buried there by his successor in the see.

[A.D. 1108—1114.] THOMAS II.; nephew of Archbishop Thomas of Bayeux. His brother, Richard, was Bishop of Bayeux from 1108 to 1133. Thomas refused to make the submission to Archbishop Anselm, without which Anselm would not consecrate him, and it was only after Anselm's death that, very unwillingly, and on the insistance of the King, he submitted, and was consecrated by the Bishop of London. Little is recorded of this Archbishop, who died at Beverley in 1114.

[1114—1140.] THURSTAN, his successor, was one of the most

---

[f] For the curious story of their restoration, see Symeon of Durham; and Mabillon, ' Annales Bened.', vol. v. 84-257.

remarkable of the northern archbishops. Like other great churchmen of his time, he was the son of a priest. His father's name was Auger, a Prebendary of London. Auger was a native of Bayeux ; and had another son, Andoenus (Ouen), who became Bishop of Evreux. Thurstan had belonged to the household of William Rufus, and on that King's death became the Chaplain and Secretary of Henry I., by whom he was nominated the successor of Archbishop Thomas in 1114. At this time Thurstan was only a sub-deacon. He was ordained deacon by William Giffard, Bishop of Winchester, and was then solemnly enthroned in the minster at York. The following five years were occupied in the great dispute between York and Canterbury. Thurstan steadily refused to make the required submission to the southern primate ; and Archbishop Ralph d'Escures, who in the same year, 1114, was translated from Rochester to Canterbury, refused as steadily to consecrate him without it. Thurstan was, however, ordained priest by Flambard, Bishop of Durham. The King himself supported either side in turn ; and on one occasion Thurstan resigned into his hands, as suzerain, all the preferment that he possessed. This was afterwards restored ; but in spite of the support and influence of three successive popes—Paschal, Gelasius II. (who died in 1118), and Calixtus II., all of whom were favourable to Thurstan, Archbishop Ralph persisted in his refusal, and Thurstan was at length consecrated during the Council of Rheims (Oct. 20, 1119), by the hands of Calixtus himself. Henry disseised Thurstan of the archiepiscopal lands ; and the new archbishop remained for some months in the Papal Court, until Calixtus, determining that the Church of York should be for ever freed from the profession to Canterbury, gave Thurstan a charter of exemption to that effect with the papal bull affixed, and despatched him toward England with letters threatening Henry with excommunication if the Archbishop were not at once placed in his see. Thurstan, with the Papal Ambassadors, the

Archbishop of Tours, and the Bishop of Beauvais, found Henry in Normandy ; and after some debate it was agreed that the temporalities should be restored to Thurstan, if he would still remain absent for a time from England. Thurstan consented ; and Henry sailed from Barfleur (Nov. 25, 1120), his son following him in the 'White Ship,' which was lost with all on board. At Christmas the King summoned the Archbishop of Canterbury and his suffragans, and showed them the letters and mandates of Calixtus. They did not venture to disobey them, and Thurstan was invited to cross the sea. Early in the spring of 1121 he was received at York by vast multitudes who thronged out of the city to meet him, and was re-enthroned in the minster. The claims of Canterbury were, however, by no means extinguished. They were revived, and before the Pope, by Ralph's successor, William de Corbeil; and were only placed in abeyance for a time by the appointment of Corbeil as Papal Legate in England, thus giving him personally an undisputed superiority.

As Archbishop of York, Thurstan is especially noticeable for the part he took in 1138, on the occasion of the battle of the Standard, and as the great patron of monasticism in the north of England. In 1137 he had visited Scotland as ambassador, and had induced King David to make a truce with England until the return of Stephen from abroad. But in the following year the Scots broke into Northumberland, and thence advanced as far as the neighbourhood of Northallerton in Yorkshire. The English army which met them there was assembled mainly by the exertions of the Archbishop; and the result of the battle was the entire defeat of the Scots, and the safety of the north of England. The "Standard," from which the field was named, was a wheeled platform, resembling the "Carrocio," used for the same purpose in Italy. On it were raised the holy banners of St. Peter of York, St. John of Beverley, and St. Wilfrid of Ripon. (The historians of the

'Bellum Standardi' are Ailred of Rievaulx, whose narrative
is printed in Twysden's 'Decem Scriptores,' and Richard
of Hexham, whose history is also printed in the 'Decem
Scriptores,' and has been recently edited by Canon Raine
for the Surtees Society.)

As a great reviver of monasticism Thurstan is almost
entitled to rank with St. Bernard, his personal friend and
correspondent. At the time of Thurstan's accession to the
see of York there were few religious houses in the north of
England, the only orders being Benedictines, Augustinian
Canons, and Cluniacs, the last of whom had one monastery
only, at Pontefract. During his episcopate, six new houses
of Augustinians were established in Yorkshire—Kirkham,
Gisborough, Bridlington, Bolton, Nostel and Drax; and the
great order of Reformed Benedictines—the Cistercians—
were first introduced. The Cistercian houses of Rievaulx, of
Byland, and of Fountains, were founded and fostered at the
especial instance of Thurstan; and it is probable that the
monks who colonized Rievaulx had been sent into Yorkshire by St. Bernard himself, in the hope that Thurstan
would provide them with a resting-place. The site of
Fountains had been the Archbishop's own property.

A few days before his death, Thurstan, in accordance
with the advice of St. Bernard, and in fulfilment of a vow
made at Clugny in his youth, became a monk among the
Cluniacs at Pontefract. He died Feb. 5, 1140, and was
buried before the high altar of the Cluniac Church.

On the death of Thurstan, the Chapter of York first
chose as his successor, at the instance of Henry of Blois,
the powerful Bishop of Winchester, his nephew, Henry
de Sully, Abbot of Fécamp. The Pope, however, refused
to recognise him, because he would not give up his monastery; and in January, 1141-42, the Chapter chose
[A.D. 1143—deprived 1147—restored 1153, died 1154—
WILLIAM FITZHERBERT, afterwards known as St. WILLIAM
OF YORK.] His father, Count Herbert, had been Chamber-

1

lain and Treasurer to Henry I. His mother, Emma, was
a grand-daughter of the Conqueror, and sister of King
Stephen. Either because, as was asserted, Court influence had been strongly brought to bear on his election, or
for some other reason which is nowhere made clearly evident, the election of William was violently opposed by the
party of reformers in the Church, and especially by the
Cistercians. The accusations against William were heard
at Rome, by Pope Innocent, and a judgment was so far
given in his favour that his consecration was permitted,
provided the Dean of York would state on oath that no
undue influence had been exerted on the part of the King.
This was done, not by the Dean, Hugh de Puiset, himself,
who meanwhile had become Bishop elect of Durham, but
by the Bishop of Orkney, and the Abbots of St. Mary's
and Whitby on his behalf; and William was consecrated
at Winchester, Sept. 26, 1143, by his uncle, Henry of Blois.
In 1145 the pall was sent to him by Pope Lucius, who
died in the same year. His successor was the Cistercian
Pope Eugenius III. The archbishop's pall had not yet
been delivered. The Cistercians, encouraged by St. Bernard, revived the old charges. Archbishop William himself went to Rome. The cause was again tried, and the
Pope suspended the Archbishop until the late Dean of York
should himself take the required oath. Meanwhile certain
followers of William, enraged at the treatment he was
receiving from the Cistercians, attacked, plundered, and
burnt the monastery of Fountains. The Pope became altogether hostile, and at a council held at Rheims, in 1147,
deprived William of his see.

[A.D. 1147—1153.] HENRY MURDAC, Abbot of Fountains,
the friend and close follower of St. Bernard, was elected in
his place. Murdac was a stern and austere reformer. It
was not until 1151 that the King, Stephen, would receive
him; but in that year a reconciliation took place, and
Murdac was sent to Rome, to procure from Pope Eugenius

a formal recognition of the right of Eustace, son of Stephen, to the throne of England. The election of Hugh de Puiset to the see of Durham was strongly opposed by Archbishop Murdac, because, as he asserted, besides the unfitness of the choice, the metropolitan ought to have been consulted before the election was made; and the Prior and Arch- deacon of Durham were only allowed to receive him as bishop after they had submitted themselves to Murdac's authority, and had been publicly scourged at the entrance of Beverley Minster. Murdac died at Beverley, Oct. 14, 1153. The Cistercian Pope, Eugenius, and St. Bernard died in the same year. With them, Murdac is recorded in the Chronicle of Fountains, " Dilexerunt se invicem in vita sua, in morte non separati, duces gregis Domini, columnæ domus Dei, luminaria mundi."

[A.D. 1153—1154]. After his deposition, Archbishop William found an asylum in the palace of his uncle at Winchester. There he is said to have won all hearts by the gentleness and patience with which he bore his troubles. The chap- ter of York re-elected him on Murdac's death. He went himself to plead his cause at Rome; where the new Pope, Anastasius, accepted his election, and gave him the pall. He was received at York on his return by a vast and re- joicing crowd, but as the procession was crossing the Ouse by a wooden bridge it gave way, and great numbers fell into the river. William is said to have saved them by a miracle; and a chapel dedicated to him was afterwards built on the bridge of stone erected in the same place, The Archbishop was in York but thirty days. He cele- brated mass on Trinity Sunday, but was taken ill during the service, and died within a week. It was said that poison had been mixed with the sacramental wine; but there is no evidence whatever of this, and it seems toler- ably certain that he died of rapid fever.

The church of York had as yet no saint peculiar to itself, and was accordingly most anxious to procure the canonization of Archbishop William. This was not effected, however, until the pontificate of Nicholas III. when the " money and urgent entreaties " of Anthony Bek, the magnificent Bishop of Durham (then only bishop elect), brought about the papal assent. For the translation and the shrine of St. William, see Pt. I. § xvi..

Two hymns addressed to him are printed by Canon Raine; one of which refers curiously to the belief that he was poisoned in the chalice :—

> " In octavis Penthecostes
> Quidam malignantes hostes,
> In eum pacifice,
> Et ut ipsum privent vita—
> Celebrantis achonita
> Propinat in calice.
> Toxicatur a prophanis
> Ille potus ille panis
> Per quem perit toxicum.
> Ambo presul amplexatur,
> Et per unum moriatur
> Et vivat per reliquum."

[A.D. 1154—1181.] ROGER DE PONT L'EVÊQUE, the successor of St. William, had been long in the "familia" of Archbishop Theobald of Canterbury, before, in 1148, he became Archdeacon of Canterbury. His election in 1154 to the see of York seems to have been brought about by the influence of Archbishop Theobald.

During the struggle between Henry II. and Archbishop Becket, Roger took the King's side, and was consequently described by Becket as "malorum omnium incentor et caput," and even as "diabolus ille." In 1170, Roger, in conjunction with the Bishops of Durham, London, Salisbury, and Rochester, crowned Prince Henry King of England. This was the step against which Becket so violently protested, as an interference with his acknowledged right. At his request the Pope suspended Archbishop Roger and his suffragan, the Bishop of Durham, and excommunicated the southern prelates. Roger crossed the Channel to Henry, with the Bishops of London and Salisbury, and it was after his representations to the King that Henry uttered the famous speech which led to the murder of Becket. Roger afterwards swore that he was entirely innocent of that murder; but the partizans of Canterbury held that he was one of the chief causes of Becket's misfortunes; and in 1176, at the Council of Westminster, they took special vengeance on him. The papal legate Huguccio was present at the Council, and it was a question which of the Archbishops was entitled to sit on his right hand. Richard of Canterbury had taken the place, when "York," entering, is said to have sat down in "Canterbury's" lap. The friends of Canterbury immediately seized him, threw him down, beat him and trampled on him, tore his cope, and dismissed him, with the cry "Away! away, betrayer of St. Thomas! His blood is still upon thy hands!" Archbishop Roger obtained no redress.

Roger, who was one of the leading politicians of his time, was a man of learning and ability, the friend of John of Salisbury, of Gilbert Foliot, and of many other scholars. According to William of Newburgh he was violently opposed to the monastic system, and especially to the Cistercians, saying that Thurstan's greatest error had been the establishment of Fountains. For his own diocese he did much. He rebuilt nearly all his archiepiscopal residences, including the palace of York on the north side of the Cathedral. The choir of the minster was also rebuilt by him, and he began "de novo" the building of St. Wilfrid's "basilica" at Ripon. (See that Cathedral, Pt I. § i.) At the death of Archbishop Roger in 1181, the King (Henry II.), on the ground that he had died intestate, seized the whole of his money and plate, amounting in value to 11,000*l.* He was buried by Hugh de Puiset, Bishop of Durham, in the choir of his own Cathedral. (See Pt. I. § vi. *note.*)

For ten years the see of York remained vacant, whilst the revenues passed into the royal coffers. The Archbishop who at last succeeded Roger was

[A.D. 1191—1207.] GEOFFRY PLANTAGENET, an illegitimate son of Henry II.; it is said that his mother was Rosamond Clifford, the "Fair Rosamond" of story. Geoffry, whose "tumultuous nature" is insisted upon by Fuller, inherited a full measure of the stormy Plantagenet character. When still a child he was made Archdeacon of Lincoln, and when about fourteen his father procured his election to the bishopric of that see. The Pope refused to consecrate him for three years; but the Bishop elect, who was not even in priest's orders, received all the temporalities until 1181, when the Pope, Alexander III., insisted that he should either receive ordination or give up Lincoln altogether. He chose the latter, receiving in exchange from the King many rents and offices in England and Normandy. Alone of Henry's sons, Geoffry was faithful to his father, and was with him at his death in the Castle of Chinon, in 1189. On his return to England, Geoffry was met in London by a body of the York ecclesiastics, informing him that he had been elected to that see, which had been so long vacant. At first he declined positively, telling them that he was fonder of dogs and hawks than of books and priests. They answered that his tastes need not be altogether abandoned when he came into the north as Archbishop; and Geoffry at last consented to accept their nomination, which was shortly afterwards confirmed by Richard I. Geoffry was then ordained priest; but it was not until the 18th of August, 1191, that he was consecrated Bishop in the Church of St. Maurice at Tours by the Archbishop of that see. There had already been dissension between Geoffry and Richard; and, before leaving for the Holy Land, Richard is said to have extorted a promise from both his brothers, John and Geoffry, that they would not return to England for three years after his departure without his special permission. However this may be, Geoffry returned at once after his consecration, and at Dover was seized by order of the Bishop of Ely, Grand Justiciar of the Kingdom in Richard's absence. For some days he was imprisoned in the Castle; but the Bishop of Ely was at length compelled to let the Archbishop go without swearing the allegiance on which he had insisted. Geoffry at once proceeded to York.

The canons there seem to have discovered at once that their choice had been an imprudent one. Throughout Geoffry's episcopate he was in constant dissension either with them or with his brothers, Richard and John. The Pope, Celestine, at the instance of the canons, issued a commission of inquiry in 1195, at the head of which was the Bishop of Lincoln. The result was, the suspension of Archbishop Geoffry by the Pope; but that suspension was reversed, and a sentence given altogether in Geoffry's favour on his personal appeal to Rome. Sometimes in great favour with John, and sometimes deprived of all his temporalities except the manor of Ripon, Geoffry continued to hold the see of York until 1207, when John extorted from his subjects the tax of a thirteenth, and Geoffry set his face stoutly against it. He excommunicated all those who should attempt to collect it in his province; and then was compelled to provide for his own safety by flight. He never returned to England; and died, it is said, in 1212 at Grosmont in Normandy.

After Geoffry's flight the temporalities of the archbishopric remained in the King's hands until
[A.D. 1216—1255.] WALTER DE GRAY was nominated to the see, which had thus been vacant for nine years.

The family of De Gray was one of considerable importance, and is still represented on the roll of peers. The future Archbishop was educated at Oxford, and was early brought to the notice of King John, to whom he was indebted for all his preferments. In 1207 he was made a prebendary of Rochester, and in the same year received a stall at Exeter and the archdeaconry of Totnes. Many other appointments followed; and in 1288 he was elected Bishop of Lichfield and Coventry by the Chapter of Lichfield, in opposition to the nominee of the monks of Coventry. The legate Pandulph would admit neither, and a third person at length became the prelate. In October, 1214, however, De Gray was consecrated Bishop of Worcester, resigning all his former preferments. The Chapter of York had elected Simon Langton, brother of the famous Archbishop of Canterbury, to their vacant see; but the King would not receive him, and the Pope, Innocent III., at once set him aside when the Canons of York sent their representatives to Rome. The Canons, prepared for such an emergency, then nominated Walter de Gray, Bishop of Worcester, who was at time also in Rome. The Pope accepted him; and De Gray returned, with the pall, to England. It is said that he paid 10,000*l.* for the papal recognition.

De Gray was a marked favourite with both John and Henry III., and was, beyond a doubt, the most distinguished English prelate of his time. He is said to have complied readily with all the wishes of King John,[g] and was certainly on the King's side during the great struggle for the Magna Charta. Under Henry III. De Gray was frequently employed on important diplomatic services. In 1227 he was sent to France, in the hope of inducing the great lords of Normandy, Anjou, Brittany, and Poictou to accept Henry as their suzerain; and in 1237 he was sent with the Earl of Cornwall to an assembly convened by the Emperor Frederick. Archbishop De Gray was appointed regent of the kingdom during Henry's absence in France in 1242, and was again regent in 1254, when the Queen joined her husband in Gascony. In every important event

[g] In omnibus regni agendis regis studuit facere voluntatem.— *M. Paris*, 192.

which took place in the history of the nation the Archbishop of York was more or less concerned. He several times entertained the Kings of England and Scotland, with their Queens, at York; the most memorable occasion being in 1252, when the English court and the royal house of Scotland kept their Christmas at York, and the young King, Alexander III., then eight years old, was married to Henry's daughter Margaret. In 1255 De Gray was present at a parliament which in effect ushered in the war of the barons. The whole country was in a state of sullen indignation, and on the dissolution of the parliament the Archbishop retired to the Bishop of London's palace at Fulham. He had been there only three days when he died, May 1, 1255.

In his own diocese Walter de Gray was a great benefactor. He found it in a state of utter neglect, and left it at his death in comparative wealth and order. He purchased and annexed to the stalls and offices of the Chapter many churches and livings. He bought and appropriated to the see the village of St. Andrewthorpe, the name of which was speedily changed to Bishopthorpe, from the palace which he built there, and which is still the residence of the Archbishops. In London he bought York House for the see, to which it remained attached until Henry VIII. compelled Wolsey to resign it, and its name was changed to Whitehall. De Gray built the south transept of his minster (Part I., § III.), and his tomb remains there (Part I., § VI.), the place of his interment having probably been chosen by himself. At Ripon he probably built the west front of the existing cathedral, and translated the relics of St. Wilfrid. (See *Ripon Cathedral*, Part I., §§ I., XI.)

[A.D. 1256—1258.] SEWAL DE BOVILL, Dean of York, was Gray's successor. He had been educated at Oxford, where he had sat at the feet of Edmund of Abingdon, afterwards the canonised Archbishop of Canterbury. St. Edmund is said to have predicted the future elevation of Archbishop Sewal; and the Archbishop himself afterwards wrote to Innocent IV., urging him to canonise his old instructor. Matthew Paris speaks highly of Archbishop Sewal's modesty, piety, and learning. A long and remarkable letter, addressed to him after his elevation by the Franciscan Adam de Marisco, holding up to him Grostête of Lincoln as a pattern, will be found in the *Monumenta Franciscana.*[h]

The only noticeable event of Sewal's episcopate is his quarrel with the Pope on account of the deanery of York. Geoffry of Ludham had been appointed, but the Pope bestowed the deanery on a certain Italian named Jordan, who was installed by an ingenious trick. Bovill resisted steadily; the Pope suspended him, put the minster under an interdict, and at length excommunicated both the Archbishop and Dean Geoffry. It does not appear that the excommunication was ever removed; at any rate, the Archbishop sank under his troubles, and died May 10, 1258. He was buried in the south transept, near his predecessor (Part I., § VI).

[A.D. 1258—1265] GEOFFREY OF LUDHAM, OR OF KINTON (taking his names probably from the villages of Loudham and Kinalton, or Kinston, in Nottinghamshire), succeeded. He had been Bovill's Dean of York, and had been excommunicated with the Archbishop. His sentence must soon, however, have been removed; since on his election to the see he went himself to Rome, and, after much trouble and expense, was consecrated there and returned with the pall. As Archbishop he was not very prominent. Little is known of him, and the chroniclers are silent.

On the death of Ludham the Chapter again fixed on their Dean, William Langton. The Pope refused to accept him, and nominated instead Bonaventura, the famous

[h] In the series of Chronicles published under the direction of the Master of the Rolls.

Franciscan, who refused the appointment. After the see had been vacant for twelve months the Pope, Clement IV., promoted to it

[A.D. 1266—1279.] WALTER GIFFARD, member of a wealthy and powerful family of Boyton, in Wiltshire. Little is known of his early history. In 1264 he became Bishop of Bath and Wells, and was Lord Chancellor of England in 1265, resigning that office on his translation to York. He was a great favourite with Edward I., who, when starting on the crusade in 1270, drew up his will, in which he made Giffard one of the tutors of his sons. In 1275 he was one of those to whom the charge of the kingdom was entrusted during Edward's absence.

Archbishop Giffard is recorded in the Lanercost Chronicle as "formosus et illustris clericus," and in another place as "socialis et dapsilis." He was greatly in debt throughout the whole course of his episcopate; but was certainly most charitable, full of attention to his diocese, and a fearless reformer of abuses. His register, preserved at York, is full of information relating to the ecclesiastical state of the north of England, and contains curious details of the Archbishop's private charities and expenditure. Giffard's tomb, in the choir, was removed to the presbytery by Archbishop Thoresby (Part I. § XVIII.).

[A.D. 1279—1285.] WILLIAM OF WICKWAINE succeeded. Of his family and early life nothing is known. He had been Chancellor of York, and on his election went to Rome to receive the pall. The Pope set aside his election by the Chapter, but appointed him by his own authority to the vacant see, and consecrated him at Viterbo, Sept. 19, 1279. Wickwaine had little to do with affairs of state, and devoted his whole time to the most active care of his diocese. He was a severe and strict disciplinarian, with the heart of a true monk, and did his best to restore discipline in the monasteries, which had greatly fallen away from order. He attempted to visit the priory of

Durham; but the prior and monks strenuously resisted, and the contest went on for the remainder of Wickwaine's life. In 1283 he was himself at Durham, and in St. Nicholas Church was on the point of excommunicating the prior and his adherents, when a tumult took place, and the Archbishop, escaping with difficulty, found a sanctuary in the hospital of Kepier. The following year he set out for Rome, in the hope of bringing the papal thunders to bear on the offenders. Either on his way or on his return (it is uncertain whether he ever reached Rome) he halted at the famous Cistercian house of Pontigny, in Burgundy, where Becket had been sheltered and where St. Edmund of Canterbury had died. There Archbishop Wickwaine also died, August 26, 1285. He was buried in the church, and miracles were said to have been wrought at his tomb. He was never canonised.

Archbishop Wickwaine translated the relics of St. William, and consecrated on the same day Anthony Bek to the bishopric of Durham (Pt. I. § xvi.).

[A.D. 1286—1296.] JOHN ROMANUS, or LE ROMEYN, was the son of the Treasurer of York, who had built the north transept and the central tower of the Minster (Pt. I., § VIII.). He had been Chancellor and Precentor of Lincoln and a Prebendary of York. Romanus was consecrated at Rome by the Pope, Feb. 10, 1285-6.

As Archbishop he "surpassed all his predecessors in his hospitality and munificence."[1] He began the construction of the present nave of his cathedral (Pt. I., § IX.), and is distinguished for the strong opposition he made to the appointment by Pope Nicholas III. of his nephew, Matthew Rubens, to the stall of Fenton, in the church of York. The Pope dropped his scheme in consequence of the vigorous letters of the King, Edward I., and the Archbishop. Romanus was hotheaded and indiscreet, and was

[1] Raine.

in perpetual dispute with his chapter. He attempted to bring the powerful Bishop of Durham (Anthony Bek) to acknowledge his subjection to the see of York; and, on Bek's resistance, went himself to the Pope, and sent from Viterbo an order for the excommunication of Bek. This was carried into effect; but Edward I. took the side of Bek, the dispute was brought before Parliament, and the decision was against Romanus, who was committed to the Tower for his offence,—not against the Bishop of Durham, but against the Prince Palatine. The Archbishop was released on payment of a fine of 4000 marks. Romanus died suddenly at Burton, near Beverley, March 11, 1296.

[A.D. 1298—1299.] HENRY OF NEWARK, Dean of York, received the temporalities in 1297, but was not consecrated until June 15, 1298. He had long been connected with the Court, and had been a clerk and chaplain of Edward I., by whom he was constantly employed in public affairs. Little is recorded of his life as Archbishop.

[A.D. 1300—1304.] THOMAS OF CORBRIDGE, "omnium artium liberalium professor incomparabilis," according to Stubbes, was Newark's successor. He had been Chancellor of York, and afterwards Sacrist of the Chapel of St. Sepulchre, adjoining the Minster; and was consecrated at Rome by Boniface VIII.; who obliged him to resign the election by the Chapter, and to receive the archbishopric from the hands of the Pope. Corbridge came more than once into collision with the King, Edward I., but little is recorded of him, and he seems to have taken no part in public affairs. He died at Laneham in Nottinghamshire, and was buried in the Collegiate Church of Southwell. His brass has disappeared, but the matrix remains.

[A.D. 1306—1315.] WILLIAM GRENFEUD, or GREENFIELD, was the first of a succession of very distinguished prelates who presided over the northern diocese, and were great English statesmen, throughout the fourteenth century. Archbishop Greenfield's birth-place is unknown; but he

was related to his predecessor in the see, Archbishop
Giffard, at whose expense he was educated at Oxford. Besides other preferments, he was, before his election to York,
Dean of Chichester, Rector of Stratford-on-Avon, and tem-
poral Chancellor of Durham. Since the year 1290 he had
been much employed in the service of the State by Edward I. ; and in 1302 he became Chancellor of England,
an office which he held for three years. Greenfield was
elected by the Chapter of York, Dec. 4, 1304; but in consequence of the death of the Pope, Benedict X., some
time elapsed before his consecration. He was at length
consecrated by Clement V. at Lyons, Jan. 30, 1306. He
had been for some time resident at Rome, where the cost
of his living and the sum spent in procuring the Papal
assent were enormous. Greenfield was obliged to borrow
money in all directions. " All the money lenders were
ecclesiastics. The Jews had disappeared some years before,
and the greater part of the treasure of the country was now
stored away in the chests of some wealthy clerk, or in the
coffers of the monastery." [k]

The war with Scotland rendered York at this time
almost the capital of England. Parliaments were held
there in 1298, 1299, and 1300; and the Courts of Justice
were removed to York, and did not return to London for
seven years. Greenfield constantly entertained Edward I.
and Edward II. in his palaces at York and at Bishopthorpe,
and had not only to supply men for the Scottish expedi-
tions, but, in conjunction with the Bishop of Durham, to
protect the eastern marches. In 1306 the Archbishop of
York and the Bishop of Lichfield were made Guardians of
the Kingdom, during the expedition of Edward I., which
was broken up on his death at Brugh-on-the Sands.

The attack on the Templars in England began in 1308,
when they and their property were taken possession of by

[k] Raine.

the royal officers. Greenfield was favourable to them, and refused altogether to take any part against them within the province of Canterbury. In 1310 a council of the northern province was assembled to inquire into the charges against them. Little or nothing was proved; but a second council was held in 1311, at which it was ordered that the twenty-four Templars who had been confined in the Castle of York since the autumn of 1309 should be sent to different religious houses within the province of York to do penance for their errors.[1]. They remained in these monasteries for the remainder of their lives. In 1319 the Pope granted permission to such of them as chose, to take the vows required by the monastery within which each was residing; but only two seem to have done so. Archbishop Greenfield was present at the Great Council of Vienne in 1312, when Clement V. finally dissolved the Order of the Templars.

Greenfield died at Cawood, Dec. 6, 1315, and was buried in the north transept of the Minster, where his monument remains (Pt. I. § VIII.). A gold ring with a ruby was taken from the finger of the Archbishop in 1735, when the tomb was opened. It is now in the vestry.

[A.D. 1317—1340.] WILLIAM OF MELTON, born of humble parents, was a native of Melton, in the parish of Welton, about nine miles from Hull. He was a contemporary of John of Hotham, Chancellor of England and Bishop of Ely, born at Hotham, very near Melton's birth-place. The two prelates were often associated in public matters, and were the most powerful churchmen of their period in England.

[1] The charges against the Northern Templars were of the usual character, and the evidence brought to prove them was nearly worthless.—Raine's 'Lives of the Archbishops of York,' p. 371, seq. For an admirable account of the proceedings against the Templars, especially in England, see Milman's 'Latin Christianity,' vol. v.

Melton was Comptroller of the Wardrobe at the accession of Edward II., and was a pluralist of the first water at the time of his elevation to the see of York. Amongst numerous other preferments he was Archdeacon of Barnstaple and Provost of Beverley. He was elected by the Chapter of York within a month of Greenfield's death, in December, 1315; but difficulties were interposed by the Court of Rome, and he was not consecrated until September, 1317, at Avignon, by Pope John XXII. Throughout his episcopate he was actively concerned in the affairs of Scotland. In 1318, in 1319, and again in 1322, the Scots under the Black Douglas made forays into Yorkshire, devastating great part of the country, destroying churches, and sacking the richest monasteries. During the raid of 1319 the King was at the siege of Berwick, and all the better soldiery was there with him. Archbishop Melton was ordered to collect what men he could, and to lead them against the Scots. Clergy, friars, and citizens of York were accordingly gathered; and the result was the battle of Myton (Oct. 12, 1319) on the Swale, in which the English were entirely routed. The battle was called " The Chapter of Myton," from the number of clergy engaged in it. It is not certain that the Archbishop was present, but he is called the " capitaine " of the host in Barbour's ' Brus,' and elsewhere. Connected with the Scottish foray of 1322 was the battle of Boroughbridge, in which the famous Earl of Lancaster was overpowered and taken prisoner. He was led from Boroughbridge to his own castle of Pontefract, and there beheaded. Archbishop Melton had unquestionably aided him at one part of his career, and seems in consequence to have fallen into some disfavour with Edward II. In 1325, however, the King's good opinion had been recovered, since Melton then became Lord Treasurer of England. He did not desert Edward in his latter days, and certainly regarded his imprisonment with great displeasure. Nor would he be present at the coronation

of Edward III., and is said afterwards (1330) to have
been engaged in a dangerous intrigue to upset the new
government. For this he was arrested and acquitted. In
January, 1328, Melton had married, in the Minster at York,
the young King to Philippa of Hainault.

Archbishop Melton completed the nave of his Minster,
and his figure still remains above the great western portal.
He is said to have assisted largely in building the fine
church of Patrington, in Holderness, and certainly gave
much toward the fabric of Beverley. He died at Cawood,
in April, 1340, and was buried in the north aisle of the
Minster nave at York (see Pt. I. § xii.). In spite of the
troubles and devastations of his diocese—which he had
relieved to a great extent—he died very wealthy, seized
of many manors and estates. His heir was his nephew,
William of Melton, of Aston, near Sheffield, who thus
became the progenitor of one of the most powerful knightly
families in the south of Yorkshire.

On the death of Melton the Canons elected
[A.D. 1342—1352] WILLIAM LA ZOUCHE, Dean of York.
The King was anxious for the election of his Secretary,
William of Kildesby, and after the choice had fallen on
Zouche he endeavoured to set aside the election, but without
effect. After a delay of two years, Zouche was consecrated
at Avignon by Pope Clement VI., July 7, 1342.

Zouche, who is said to have been a younger son of
William Lord la Zouche, of Haringworth, in Northamptonshire, had been employed by Edward III. before his
elevation to the see, but then fell into disfavour, and was
not forgiven until the beginning of the year 1346, when
he was made one of the wardens of the marches. In this
capacity the Archbishop led one of the bodies of English
troops which defeated the Scots at the battle of Neville's
Cross, close to Durham, October 18, 1346. The King was
profuse in his thanks and praises, and the Archbishop was
desired to continue his careful watch over the border.

K

Zouche died at Cawood, and was buried before the altar of St. Edward, in the nave of the Minster. He founded, and himself began the building of a chantry adjoining the south wall of the choir. This must have been taken down when Thoresby's choir (wider than the old one) was built; and no trace of it is afterwards found, although the present office of the Chapter Clerk, at one time the vestry of the Cathedral, is thought to represent the Archbishop's chantry. (Pt. I., § XVII.).

[A.D. 1352—1373.] JOHN OF THORESBY succeeded; one of the best and most active prelates who ever filled the see of York. He was the son of Hugh of Thoresby, the owner of the hamlet of Thoresby, in Wensleydale, where the Archbishop was possibly born.

Thoresby had been in the 'familia' of Archbishop Melton, under whose patronage he obtained high clerical preferment, and was perhaps introduced to the notice of Edward III. His abilities as a lawyer ensured him rapid advance in honours and position. He was for some time the King's Proctor in the Court of Rome. In 1341 he became Master of the Rolls, holding that office till 1346. In 1343 and 1345 he had temporary charge of the Great Seal. In 1347 Clement VI. appointed him Bishop of St. David's, and in the same year Thoresby was in attendance on the King at Calais, with ninety-nine persons in his retinue. In 1349 he became Lord Chancellor of England, and was translated from St. David's to Worcester. His election to York in 1352 was unanimous, and approved by both the King and the Pope; the latter of whom, however, appointed him as of his own right, refusing to recognise the election of the Chapter. In 1355 Thoresby was one of the wardens of the Cinque Ports, and in the same year one of the regents of the kingdom during Edward's absence. He resigned the Great Seal in 1356, and thenceforth devoted himself almost entirely to the care of the northern province.

This was by no means in a satisfactory condition. The highest offices in the cathedral of York had been, since the commencement of the fourteenth century, in the hands of the Roman cardinals, who were, of course, non-resident. The deanery was held by them between 1343 and 1385. Order and discipline were consequently but little observed in the church, and the rest of the diocese was in a state but little better. "The country had been desolated by the plague and the wars, and the spirit of irreligion had crept in and established itself too securely. The people were in a state of gross ignorance, and many of the clergy, if they were disposed to work at all, were not fit to teach. Some were wandering away from their parishes in the trains of knights and nobles, or haunting, in quest of secular preferment, the purlieus of the Court. Many livings were held at the same time by one man, whilst others, through the system of papal provisions, were possessed by foreigners." [m] The power of the Roman Court in this last respect came greatly to an end before the death of Edward III. Thoresby set himself to remedy the main evils as best he might, beginning with ignorance—the greatest of them all. "He caused to be drawn up, in the form of a Catechism, a brief statement of what he deemed to be necessary for salvation, comprising the Articles of Belief, the Ten Commandments, the Seven Sacraments, the Seven Deeds of Bodily and Ghostly Mercy, the Seven Virtues, and the Seven Deadly Sins; and in this we see the first faint shadowings of an English ritual." [n] This Catechism was drawn up in Latin, for the use of the clergy, and in rude English verse, translated from the Latin by John of Taystek (Tavistock), a Benedictine of St. Mary's Abbey. Both Latin and English were issued from Cawood in November, 1357. The very remarkable English version has been printed by Mr. Halliwell in his

[m] Raine's 'Lives of the Archbishops of York,' i. 467.
[n] Id. p. 469.

'Yorkshire Anthology,' and in Raine's 'Lives of the Arch-bishops of York.'

The great differences between the sees of York and Canterbury were settled during Thoresby's episcopate. It was arranged that each primate should carry his cross erect in the province of the other; but as an acknowledg-ment of this concession, "Thoresby, within the space of two months, and each of his successors within the same period after his election, was to send a knight or a doctor of laws to offer in his name, at the shrine of St. Thomas of Canterbury, an image of gold, of the value of 40l., in the fashion of an archbishop holding a cross or some other jewel."[o] It was at this time also that the Pope, Innocent VI., "to end old divisions," made, in Fuller's words, "a new distinction—Primate of All England, and Primate of England: giving the former to Canterbury and the latter to York. Thus, when two children cry for the same apple, the indulgent father divides it betwixt them; yet so that he giveth the bigger and better part to the childe that is his darling."[p]

The great work of Archbishop Thoresby in his cathedral has been fully described (Pt. I. § xv.) He was buried before the altar of the Virgin in the Lady Chapel, the "novum opus chori" which he had constructed (Pt. I., § xviii.) During Thoresby's episcopate Walter Skirlaw, afterwards Bishop of Durham, was his private chaplain, and William of Wykeham was a prebendary of York. It is possible that both Skirlaw and Wykeham, two of the greatest builders of the age, may have been greatly influenced by the works undertaken in the Minster by Archbishop Thoresby.

[A.D. 1374—trans. 1388.] ALEXANDER NEVILLE, Canon of York and a member of one of the most powerful houses in the north, was a special favourite with Richard II. On

---

[o] Raine.　　　　　　[p] 'Church History,' Bk. III.

the rising against that King in 1386, the Archbishop of York was "appealed" of treason, and it was determined to imprison him for life in Rochester Castle. He fled, and the Pope, pitying his case, translated him to the Scottish see of St. Andrew's. But the Scots would not receive him; and for three years (until his death in 1392) he served as a parish priest in Louvain, where he was buried in the church of the Carmelites.

[A.D. 1388—trans. to Canterbury 1396.] THOMAS FITZALAN OF ARUNDELL was translated to York from Ely. He was the first of the northern primates who passed from York to Canterbury. At York he bestowed many gifts and ornaments on his church, and spent much in restoring the various palaces of the see. For his life as Archbishop of Canterbury see that cathedral, Part II.

[A.D. 1397—1398.] ROBERT WALDBY, a native of York and an Austin friar, followed the Black Prince into Aquitaine, and, after long studies at Tholouse, became professor of theology there, and was greatly distinguished for his various learning. He became successively (1387) Bishop of Aire in Gascony; (1391) Archbishop of Dublin; (1396) Bishop of Chichester; and finally Archbishop of York. He was buried at Westminster, where his brass remains, in the Chapel of St. Edmund.

[A.D. 1398—1405.] RICHARD SCROOPE, son of Richard Lord Scroope, Chancellor of England under Richard II. and the builder of the great castle of Bolton, in the North Riding, is the "Archbishop of York" of Shakespeare's 'Henry IV.' He was educated at Cambridge, and afterwards in France and Italy. At Rome he became a distinguished "advocate" in the Papal Court, and on his return to England was for some time Chancellor of the kingdom; and in 1386 was raised to the see of Lichfield, whence he was translated to York in 1398. The Archbishop had been indebted to Richard II. for all his preferments, and joined the Mowbrays, Percys, and others of the great northern barons who rose in arms against Henry IV. in 1405. They were led to disband their forces by a stratagem of the Earl of Westmorland; but the Archbishop was seized and taken to the King at Pontefract, whence he was brought to Bishopthorpe, and, together with the Earl Marshal, was condemned to death in his own hall by a certain knight named Fulthorpe. Henry IV., who was present, had commanded Chief Justice Gascoign to pronounce sentence on them; but Gascoign (himself a Yorkshireman) firmly refused, on the plea that the laws gave him no jurisdiction over the life of the prelate. The Archbishop was beheaded (June 8, 1405) in a field between York and Bishopthorpe, protesting that he " never intended evil against the person of King Henry." He was buried in his own cathedral, where offerings were long made at his tomb. (See Pt. I. § xx.)

[A.D. 1407—1423.] HENRY BOWETT succeeded, after the see had been vacant for two years and a half. The Pope in the mean time had appointed Robert Hallam to the northern primacy; but finding afterwards that Henry IV. greatly desired the elevation of Bowett, he nominated Hallam to the see of Salisbury and gave the pall to Bowett, who, in 1401, had become Bishop of Bath and Wells. In 1417, during the absence of Henry V. in France, the Scots invaded England and sat down before Berwick. The Duke of Exeter marched to the relief of the town, and Archbishop Bowett, then very old and feeble, caused himself to be carried into the camp, where his addresses are said to have greatly encouraged the English soldiers. The Scots decamped hastily in the night, leaving behind them their stores and baggage. Bowett was a great lover of hospitality, and 80 tuns of claret were consumed annually in his household. He died at Cawood, and was buried in his own cathedral. (See Pt. I. § xx.)

[A.D. 1426—translated to Canterbury Sept. 1452.) JOHN KEMP had been successively Bishop of (1419) Rochester; (1421)

Chichester; and (1421) London. The Pope had at first
nominated Richard Fleming, Bishop of Lincoln, to the see
of York; but the Canons refused to recognise any papal
nomination, and at length John Kemp was appointed with
the consent of both parties. He died in March, 1453-4,
little more than six months after his translation to Canterbury. In 1439 he was created Cardinal of St. Balbina,
and was farther raised to be Cardinal of St. Rufina on his
accession to the Primacy of All England. Hence a verse
concerning him ran—

" Bis primas, ter præses, et bis Cardine functus."

[A.D. 1452—1464.] WILLIAM BOOTH was translated to York
from Lichfield. He had been a lawyer in Gray's Inn, until,
obtaining the Chancellorship of St. Paul's, he took orders
and was speedily raised to the see of Lichfield.

[A.D. 1464—1476.] GEORGE NEVILLE, younger brother of
the great Earl of Warwick, had been appointed to the see
of Exeter in 1455, when only twenty-three years of age.
He was one of those Englishmen of noble houses by whom
the high places of the Church were at this time, for the
most part, filled; partly, it would seem (and especially in
the case of the primacy), as a result of the deliberate
determination of the Pope and the Crown to band together
the Church and the nobles " against the spiritual and civil
democracy, on one side of Wat Tyler and Jack Straw, on
the other of the extreme followers of Wycliffe." ꟴ Neville is
a striking representative of the feudal churchman. When
only fourteen years old " the nobility of his descent induced the Pope, Nicholas V., to grant him a dispensation
for holding a canonry in the church of Salisbury, together
with one in that of York." He was nominated Bishop of
Exeter at the age of twenty-three; but, as he could not be
consecrated until twenty-seven, a papal bull was granted
him for receiving the profits in the mean time. The

ꟴ Milman's ' Latin Christianity,' vi. 392.

Archbishop, like his great brother, more than once changed sides during the strife between the red rose and the white. After the final defeat and death of Henry he was detained in custody for a month or two, and was then suffered to resume all his honours. Within the year, however (1472), he was again seized at the More, in Hertfordshire,—a magnificent palace, which he had himself built and furnished with the utmost splendour. The King, Edward IV., had agreed to visit the Archbishop there, for the sake of hunting; but the day before his intended arrival sent thither to seize Neville and to take possession of all his treasure, among the rest a " mitra preciosa " of enormous value, from which a royal crown was afterwards constructed. For four years Archbishop Neville was detained in prison at Calais and at Guines, and soon after his release, in 1476, died at Blithfield.

The great feast given by Neville on his installation at York is famous in the annals of gastronomy. The list of provisions, including 330 tuns of beer, 104 tuns of wine, 80 fat oxen, 1004 sheep, 3000 geese, 100 peafowl, 4000 woodcocks, besides 8 seals and 4 porpoises, will be found in Godwin's ' De Præsulibus Angliæ.'[r]

[A.D. 1476—1480.] LAWRENCE BOOTH was translated from Durham. He was half-brother of William Booth, the predecessor of Neville. He bought and added to the see the manor of Battersea. Booth died at Southwell, and, like his brother, was buried there.

[A.D. 1480—1500.] THOMAS SCOTT, or ROTHERHAM, born at Rotherham, was educated at Cambridge. In 1467 he became Bishop of Rochester, whence, in 1471, he was translated to Lincoln. In 1474 he was made Chancellor of England, holding the office until the death of Edward IV. He was imprisoned for a short time by Richard III. for his devotion to the widowed Queen and her children. Arch-

[r] P. 695.

bishop Rotherham died at Cawood (it is said, of the plague) in 1500, and was buried in his own Cathedral. (See Pt. I. § xx.) He was the second founder of Lincoln College, Oxford; and besides restoring (almost rebuilding) the fine church of his native town, founded there the "College of Jesus" for a provost, three fellows, and six choristers—"ut ubi," in his own words, "offendi Deum in decem preceptis suis, isti decem orarent pro me."

[A.D. 1501—1507.] THOMAS SAVAGE had been Bishop successively of Rochester and London. He is said to have been a great courtier, and immoderately fond of hunting. He died at Cawood, and was buried at the Minster. (Pt. I. § xix.)

[A.D. 1508—1514.] CHRISTOPHER BAINBRIDGE was a native of the village of Hilton, near Appleby, in Westmorland, and was educated at Queen's College, Oxford, where he became provost in 1495. After other preferments he was installed Dean of York in 1503, and in 1505 was made Dean of Windsor, Master of the Rolls, and a Privy Councillor. In 1507 he became Bishop of Durham, and in the following year was translated to York. The last years of his life were passed in Italy, in the service of Henry VIII., as Ambassador to Pope Julius II., who (March, 1511) gave him a cardinal's hat with the title of St. Praxede. The Cardinal, in a fit of sudden passion, struck his house-steward, Renald of Modena, and the insult was avenged by a dose of poison. Renald fell by his own hand. Archbishop Bainbridge was buried at Rome in the English Church of St. Thomas the Martyr, where his tomb remains.

[A.D. 1514—1530.] THOMAS WOLSEY. Wolsey was consecrated to the see of Lincoln in 1514. In the same year he was translated to York. In 1522 Wolsey became Bishop of Durham,—holding that see in commendam, together with York, until the death of Fox, Bishop of Winchester, in 1522,—when he resigned Durham and succeeded to Winchester, still retaining the northern primacy.

Wolsey was created Cardinal of St. Cecilia in 1515, shortly after his elevation to York. The long list of his preferments need not be added here. It was to York that Wolsey retired after his disgrace, and at his palace of Cawood that he was arrested (Oct. 29, 1530) on a charge of high treason by his former servant, Henry Percy, then Earl of Northumberland. On the 28th of November he died in the Abbey of Leicester.

[A.D. 1531—1544.] EDWARD LEE succeeded, after the see had been vacant a little more than a year. Lee was Henry VIII.'s almoner, and had been educated at Magdalene College, Oxford. He was employed on many embassies by the King, and the inscription on his tomb in the Cathedral records him as "theologus eximius, atque in omni literarum genere longe eruditissimus, sapientia et vitæ sanctitate clarus."

[A.D. 1545—deprived 1554]. ROBERT HOLGATE was translated from Llandaff. He had been a Gilbertine monk, and after the dissolution rose into great favour at Court; Henry VIII. made him one of his chaplains, raised him to the see of Llandaff, and, after his translation to York, made him President of the Council of the North. Soon after the accession of Mary, Holgate was deprived (1554) and thrown into the Tower. In the following year he was released, and died in 1556. He was married, and the charge brought against him was, that "a certain Norman claimed the Archbishop's wife, asserting that she was his own."

[A.D. 1555—deprived 1559.] NICHOLAS HEATH had been Bishop successively of (1540) Rochester and (1543) Worcester. Under Mary, Heath was President of Wales, and at the death of Gardiner he became Chancellor of England. On the accession of Elizabeth he was deprived, as a favourer of the "old religion," and spent the rest of his life at Chobham Park in Surrey, an estate which he had bought from Queen Mary. He is called by Fuller "a meek and moderate man, carrying a court of conscience in his bosome,"* and was so much in favour with Elizabeth that she visited him " mira comitate " at Chobham. He died in 1579, and was buried in Chobham Church.

[A.D. 1561—1568.] THOMAS YOUNG succeeded after the see had been for some time vacant. He was translated to York from St. David's, to which see he had been consecrated in 1560. Little is recorded of Young, who was President of the Council of the North, and died at Sheffield, June 26, 1568. During his episcopate the great hall of the Archiepiscopal Palace at York, built by Thomas of Bayeux, after the Conquest, was entirely destroyed.

[A.D. 1570, translated to Canterbury 1576.] EDMUND GRINDAL; "a prelate most primitive in all his conversation," says Fuller; born at St. Bees, in Cumberland, and educated at Cambridge. On the accession of Elizabeth Grindal became the first Protestant Bishop of London. He was a decided Puritan. (See Canterbury Cathedral, Pt. II.)

[A.D. 1577—1588]. EDWIN SANDYS was born of a good family at Conisby in Lancashire. He became President of St. Catherine's Hall at Cambridge and was Vice-Chancellor of that University when (July, 1553) the Duke of Northumberland made Cambridge his head-quarters for a few days, and induced Sandys to support the cause of Lady Jane Grey. In consequence, he was thrown in prison, and on his subsequent release fled with his wife to Germany, where he remained until the accession of Elizabeth. He was then (1559) consecrated to the see of Worcester: whence he was translated to London in 1570, and became Archbishop of York in 1577. He died and was buried at Southwell.

[A.D. 1588—1594].] JOHN PIERS, Dean of Christ Church, Oxford; (1576) Bishop of Rochester; (1577) Bishop of

* ' Worthies,' Yorkshire.

Salisbury. When Bishop of Salisbury he preached before Queen Elizabeth on occasion of the solemn thanksgiving for the defeat of the Armada.

[A.D. 1595—1606.] MATTHEW HUTTON, translated from Durham. Hutton was descended from a family seated at Priest Hutton in Lancashire. He was educated at Cambridge, and in 1561 was appointed chaplain to Archbishop Grindal. He established a character as one of the soundest scholars and most eloquent preachers in his University, and it was probably to this that he owed his promotion to the Deanery of York in 1567. As Dean of York, Hutton was involved in a somewhat fierce quarrel with Archbishop Sandys, chiefly on the question of the validity of orders in the foreign Protestant churches. The Dean leaned decidedly to the Puritan or Protestant side; but although he was compelled to make a public submission, his interests suffered so little that in 1588 he was consecrated, at the special request of Burleigh, to the see of Durham. Thence he was translated to York in 1595. He was buried in his own Cathedral. This Archbishop was the founder of the family of Hutton of Marske, in the North Riding. A gold cup, presented to him by Queen Elizabeth, is among the treasures of Marske.

[A.D. 1606—1628.] TOBIAS MATTHEW, like his predecessor translated from Durham, of which church he had been Dean. Matthew was the son of a Bristol merchant. He was allowed to be one of the most able controversialists and one of the most eloquent preachers of his age; and, according to Harington, "was greatly beloved for his sweet conversation, friendly disposition, ... and above all, a cheerful sharpness of wit that sauced his words and behaviour."[1] He became Bishop of Durham in 1595. He died at Cawood, and was buried in York Minster, where his monument, with a long inscription, remains. (Pt. I. § xx.)

‘ Nugæ Antiquæ,’ ii.

[A.D. 1628—died Nov. 6 in the same year.] GEORGE MON-
TEIGNE. Monteigne had been Bishop successively of (1617)
Lincoln, (1621) London, and (1628) Durham, which last
see he held for about six months; and died at Cawood
almost immediately after his translation to York. He was
buried in the Church at Cawood, where his monument
still exists. Monteigne had been Chaplain to the Earl of
Essex, whom he attended on the Cadiz expedition, " being
indeed," says Fuller, " one of such personal valour, that
out of his gowne he would turn his back to no man."
When Bishop of London, " he would often pleasantly say
that of him the proverb would be verified—' Lincoln was,
and London is, and York shall be.' " ᵘ

[A.D. 1628—1631.] SAMUEL HARSNETT, born at Colchester,
was, says Fuller, " bred first scholar, then fellow, then
Master of Pembroke Hall in Cambridge. A man of great
learning, strong parts, and stout spirit." ˣ He became
(1609) Bishop of Chichester, and then (1619) of Norwich;
whence he was elevated to the see of York. " Dying un-
married, he was the better enabled for public and pious
uses," ʸ and accordingly built and endowed a grammar
school at Chigwell, in Essex, the place of his first church
preferment.

[A.D. 1632—1640.] RICHARD NEILE, born at Westminster
in 1562, was installed Dean of the Abbey Church in 1605.
He is said to have been " vir mediocriter doctus, sed pre-
dicator mirabilis." For all his earlier preferments he was
indebted to Lord Burghley. After the accession of James
he became (1608) Bishop of Rochester, and was translated
successively to (1610) Lichfield, (1613) Lincoln, (1617)
Durham, (1627) Winchester, and in 1631 became Archbishop
of York. No other English bishop has passed through so
many sees. In 1627 Neile underwent the same parliamentary censure as Laud, " for favouring Popish doctrines

ᵘ ' Worthies,' Yorkshire.   ˣ ' Worthies,' Essex.
ʸ Fuller, id.

and ceremonies." He was a great courtier; and it is of him that the story is told, how King James, asking Andrewes, Bishop of Winchester, and Neile of Durham, whether he might not take his subjects' money when he wanted it, "without all this formality in Parliament?" was answered by Neile, "God forbid Sire, but you should; you are the breath of our nostrils." "Well, my Lord of Winchester, what say you?" "Sir I have no skill to judge parliamentary cases." "No puts off," said the King, "answer me presently." "Then Sir," said Bishop Andrewes, "I think it lawful to take my brother Neile's money, for he offers it."

[A.D. 1641—1650.] JOHN WILLIAMS, translated from Lincoln; was born at Aberconway in Carnarvonshire; "well descended on both sides." The life of Archbishop Williams belongs so completely to the history of his time, that it need not be recorded here at any length. It has been amply treated by his chaplain, John Hacket, Bishop of Lichfield after the Restoration; in volumes which rank among the most valuable and amusing of the many memoirs of that time. Williams was the great rival of Laud; and was consecrated (1621) to the Bishopric of Lincoln, one week before Laud's consecration to that of St. David's. Williams was undoubtedly one of the most astute prelates who have ever presided over the northern province. He was for some time Lord Chancellor. He was deprived with the rest of the Bishops, and "after the murder of the King lived very retired, seemed to take no satisfaction in his life, and used to rise every night at midnight to his devotions."

[A.D. 1660—1664.] ACCEPTED FREWEN, sprung from an ancient family in Sussex, was educated at Magdalene College, Oxford, of which he was elected President in 1626. In 1644 he was consecrated in Magdalene Chapel to the see of Lichfield, but remained a Bishop without a diocese until the Restoration, when he was elevated to the see of York. His monument remains in the Cathedral. (Pt. I. § xx.)

[A.D. 1664—1683.] RICHARD STERNE was translated from Carlisle. He had been Master of Jesus College, Cambridge, and on account of his strong Royalist tendencies, was for some time imprisoned by the Parliament. On the restoration he became Bishop of Carlisle. Sterne was the Chaplain of Archbishop Laud, and attended him on the scaffold. He assisted Walton in the Polyglot Bible, published in 1657, and is one of those to whom the authorship of the 'Whole Duty of Man' has been attributed. The Archbishop was the great-grandfather of Lawrence Sterne, the novelist. His monument is in the north choir-aisle of the minster. (Pt. I. § XIX.)

[A.D. 1683—1686.] JOHN DOLBEN; translated from Rochester. He was student of Christ Church, Oxford, during the Civil War, and became a "Major" of the King's troops in garrison at Oxford; serving afterwards at Marston Moor (where he was standard-bearer and was severely wounded), and in the defence of York. He was ejected from Christ Church by the Parliamentarian visitors in 1648; in 1666 was consecrated Bishop of Rochester, and was translated to York in 1683. He is said to have been "a person of great natural parts," and a celebrated preacher. His tomb was in the south choir-aisle. (Pt. I. § XXI.)

[A.D. 1688—1691.] THOMAS LAMPLUGH became Bishop of Exeter in 1676; and in 1688, on the arrival of William in Tor Bay, after delivering an address in which he exhorted the people of his diocese to remain faithful to King James, he set them an unedifying example by taking flight to London. Lamplugh's adherence to James procured him the Archbishopric of York, which had been kept vacant for two years. He was confirmed in his new see before the arrival of William in London; but his Jacobitism was of no very profound character, and did not prevent him from assisting at the coronation of the Prince of Orange. He was buried in his own cathedral. (Pt. I., § XXI.)

[A.D. 1691—1714.] JOHN SHARPE, was born at Bradford, in

Yorkshire, in 1644. Under the patronage of Sir Heneage Finch he received many preferments, and became Dean of Norwich in 1681. In 1686 he was suspended for his zeal in the cause of the Church of England against that of Rome. In 1688, however, he was made one of James II.'s chaplains, and in 1689 Dean of Canterbury. He could not be persuaded to accept any one of the sees vacated by the non-juring bishops; but on the death of Lamplugh was elevated to the northern Primacy. The inscription on his monument (Pt. I. § xx.) was written by Smalridge, Bishop of Bristol.

[A.D. 1714—1724.] Sir William Dawes, son of Sir John Dawes, an Essex baronet, to whose estate and title he succeeded after the death of two brothers. He was indebted for his advancement "not to any uncommon-sized abilities," but to "the comeliness of his person, the melody of his voice, the decency of his action, and the majesty of his whole appearance." In 1708 he became Bishop of Chester, and passed to York in 1714.

[A.D. 1724—1743.] Launcelot Blackburne, translated from Exeter, to which see he was consecrated in 1717. Blackburne's youth is said to have been marked by strange experiences; and it is asserted that he was at one time a pirate. According to Anthony Wood, he matriculated at Christ Church, Oxford, in 1676; proceeded M.A. in 1683; and afterwards became chaplain to Sir Jonathan Trelawney, who was consecrated Bishop of Bristol in 1685, and was translated to Exeter in 1689. Blackburne, it is said, served as chaplain on board a buccaneering ship sent to prey on the Spaniards. Hence the charge of "piracy." If any part of his life was really so passed, it must have been between 1685 and 1691, in which latter year he was made a Canon of Exeter. In 1705 Blackburne became Dean of Exeter; and in 1717 was consecrated Bishop of that see.. In 1724 he was translated to York. His manner was always rough; and he is said, even as Archbishop, to have retained sundry vices mere appropriate to a buccaneer than a buccaneer's chaplain. It was this "jolly old Archbishop of York," as Walpole calls him, who made the well-known reply to Queen Caroline, which led to the preferment of Bishop Butler of the 'Analogy.' The Queen had asked if Butler were dead? "No, Madam," answered Blackburne—"but he is buried!" Blackburne died in London, and was buried in St. Margaret's Church, Westminster.

[A.D. 1743, translated to Canterbury, 1747.] THOMAS HERRING was translated from Bangor. As Archbishop of York, Herring is chiefly noticeable for the zeal with which he supported the cause of government during the rising of 1745. A subscription was raised in his diocese to the amount of 40,000*l*., and it was owing to this, and to the Archbishop's exertions, that the Jacobites of Yorkshire were prevented from joining the insurrection.

[A.D. 1747; translated to Canterbury, 1757.] MATTHEW HUTTON, translated from Bangor, was a member of the family which had already supplied an Archbishop to the see of York. His monument remains in the S. choir aisle. (Pt. I., (§ XXI.)

[A.D. 1757—1761.] JOHN GILBERT; Bishop (1740) of Llandaff; (1749) of Salisbury.

[A.D. 1761—1776.] ROBERT HAY DRUMMOND; Bishop (1748) of St. Asaph; (1761) of Salisbury, whence (in the same year) he was translated to York.

[A.D. 1777—1807.] WILLIAM MARKHAM, translated from Chester.

[A.D. 1808—1847.] E. V. VERNON HARCOURT; translated from Carlisle.

[A.D. 1847—1860.] THOMAS MUSGRAVE, translated from Hereford.

[A.D. 1860, translated to Canterbury, 1862.] CHARLES F. LONGLEY, translated from Ripon.

[A.D. 1862.] WILLIAM THOMSON; translated from Gloucester.

L

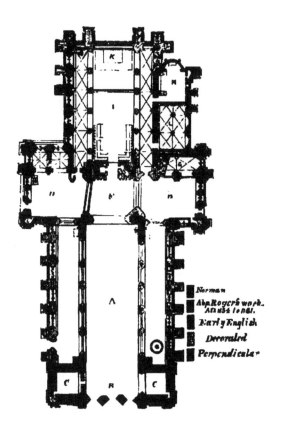

Norman
Abp Rogers work.
An 1154 to 1181.
Early English
Decorated
Perpendicular

REFERENCES.

A *Nave.*
B *West Entrance.*
C C *Western Towers.*
D D *Transept.*
E *Central Tower.*
F *Aisle of North Transept.*
G *Aisle of South Transept.*
H *Steps to Lady Loft.*
I *Choir.*
K *Altar.*
L *Chapter House.*
M *Vestry.*
N *Entrance to Crypt, called St. Wilfrid's Needle.*
O *Probable position of the Shrine of St. Wilfrid.*

GROUND PLAN OF RIPON CATHEDRAL

Scale of 100 feet to 1 inch

RIPON CATHEDRAL.

CORBEL IN SOUTH AISLE OF CHOIR.

RIPON CATHEDRAL WEST FRONT.

RIPON CATHEDRAL.

———◦∞◦———

PART I.

History and Details.

I. For the earlier history of Ripon, see Part II.[a] It
is only necessary to say here that St. Wilfrid, after his
consecration to the Northumbrian see in the year 664,
erected a "Basilica" at Ripon.[b] This basilica was
the church of a monastery, over which Wilfrid afterwards presided. It was not on the site of the existing
cathedral; but there is the strongest reason for believing
that Wilfrid founded a second church in Ripon on that
site, and that the crypt below the present nave was
connected with this second foundation. (See *post*
§ xiv.) Odo, Archbishop of Canterbury (942—959),
visited the northern province soon after the year

---

[a] The history of Ripon Cathedral has been most fully and
carefully treated by John Richard Walbran, Esq., F.S.A., in his
local guide (Harrison, Ripon), and in papers communicated to
the Archæological Institute. Mr. Walbran has done so much
for Ripon, that little is left for those who follow him but to
condense his descriptions.

[b] Eddius, Vita Wilfridi. (See Part II.)

948,[c] when King Eadred " harried" Northumbria, and burnt Wilfrid's monastery; and Leland was assured that the "commune opinion" in his time was, that Odo then " took pitie on the desolation of Ripon Church, and began, or caused a new work to be edified wher the minstre now is."[d] Of this structure, he adds, no part remained. It may have been altogether removed, or a portion of it only may have been rebuilt, soon after the Conquest; it is at least certain that a church, containing much Norman work, existed on this site before Roger de Pont l'Evêque, Archbishop of York (1154—1181) began the existing structure, with which he incorporated some portion of the older building.[e] For the subsequent history of the church there is, so far as is known, not much documentary evidence. Archbishop Walter Gray (1215—1255) probably added the west front. Toward the end of the thirteenth century (1288—1300) the eastern portion of the choir was rebuilt, the work of Archbishop Roger being replaced by two decorated bays. The Scots set fire to

[c] This is the date given in the Saxon chronicle. Simeon of Durham assigns the "harrying" to the year 950. According to Leland, Odo accompanied Eadred.

[d] Itin. i. 91.

[e] That Archbishop Roger began the rebuilding of the church, and provided for its completion, appears from his own statement, "quod dedimus operi beati Wilfridi de Ripon ad ædificandam basilicam ipsius quam *de novo inchoavimus* mille libras veteris monetæ." The discovery of this record is due to Mr. Walbran. Archbishop Roger rebuilt the choir of York Minster (see that Cathedral, Part I. § 1.) and the Archiepiscopal palace there. Of this latter some portions remain.

the church in 1319; and some restoration (for the most part, probably, of wood-work) was required after their foray. About the year 1454 the central tower had become greatly ruined, and part of it had fallen. It was then rebuilt; and during the first years of the sixteenth century Archbishop Roger's nave was removed, and Perpendicular work substituted for it. The wooden spire above the central tower had been struck by lightning in 1593; and in 1660 it was blown down, demolishing in its fall the roof of the choir. This was restored; and the spires of the western towers were then removed in fear of a similar calamity. In 1829 the nave was new-roofed and ceiled, and the choir groined with lath and plaster, happily now removed. In 1862 the building was placed in the hands of Mr. G. G. Scott for a complete restoration, which has been effected with the utmost skill, and with (unless the removal of the mullions from the windows of the west front (§ III.) must be excepted) the strictest preservation of every antique fragment.

The Manor of Ripon was bestowed by the Conqueror on Thomas of Bayeux, the first Norman Archbishop of York. It was long a favourite residence of the Archbishops, to whose care and outlay the flourishing condition of the Minster was greatly owing. A body of Augustinian canons, called "Canons of St. Wilfrid," was attached to the Minster until the dissolution.[f] In

---

[f] The Augustinians had possibly been introduced by Aldred, Archbishop of York, between 1060 and 1069. They were in possession at the time of the Domesday survey.

1604 James I. erected it into a collegiate church, with a dean and six prebendaries; and in this condition it remained until, in 1836, the Church and Chapter became the Cathedral and Chapter of the new diocese of Ripon.

II. In accordance with the dates already mentioned, the Minster exhibits—

Saxon (*probably Wilfrid's work*)—crypt.

Norman (Archbishop Thomas? 1070—1100)—Portions of Chapter-house and crypt below it.

Transition-work (Archbishop Roger, 1154—1181)—Transepts; three bays north side of choir; portions of nave piers adjoining the west and central towers.

Early English (1215—1255)—West front and west towers; vaulting and circular windows of Chapterhouse.

Early Decorated (*Geometrical*) (1288—1300)—Two easternmost bays of choir.

Perpendicular (1460—1520)—South and east sides of central tower; east side of main wall of south transept; choir-screen; two bays south side of choir; nave.

The older portion of the cathedral (Roger's work and the west front) is built of grit stone from Pately Bridge or from the neighbourhood of Brimham Crags. The Perpendicular work is of magnesian limestone; and for the late restorations both sandstone grit and limestone have been used.

III. The Minster is approached from the market-place by the narrow Kirkgate, at the end of which

PLATE I.

RIPON CATHEDRAL.

WINDOWS IN THE WEST FRONT, RIPON CATHEDRAL.

AS THEY WERE BEFORE THE "RESTORATION."

rises the beautiful *west front*. (Frontispiece. In this view some of the intervening houses are supposed to be removed, so as to show the entire front.) This front, Archbishop Gray's addition to Archbishop Roger's church, is a singularly pure example of Early English. It consists of a central gable, 103 feet high, between flanking towers of somewhat greater elevation. The towers are divided from the central compartment by flat unstaged buttresses, rising quite to the top. Although they project but slightly, these buttresses give considerable relief to the front, the whole of which is on the same plane. In the central compartments are three portals, receding in five orders, with double shafts (one behind the other—an arrangement occurring at Lincoln, and in the Galilee porch at Ely), much dog-tooth ornament, and gabled pediments. The shafts in front are without bases. Above are five pointed windows of equal height, which, until the late restoration, had quatrefoils in the heading, and were divided by mullions. These, it is true, were no part of the original design, but they were ancient insertions of Early English character, apparently of not much later date than the rest of the front; and their removal is a very doubtful improvement. (Plate I. The windows are here shown as they were before the restoration. The details of shafts and mouldings of course remain.) There is a small niche with a figure remaining in it, above one of these windows. The figure is so weather-worn that its characteristics are quite lost. Above, again, are five lancets; that in the centre, from which the others decline, being the highest ; and in the gable are three narrow lights, the central being the highest, with a blind trefoil in the wall above. Much dog-tooth ornament occurs in the mouldings of all these windows; but the capitals of the lower tier are foliated, those of the upper, plain ; and generally it should be remarked that the ornamentation becomes less from the portals upward. The towers have buttresses at each angle. The shafts at the angles of the buttresses terminate in capitals, and deserve notice. Each tower is divided by string-courses into four stages, the lowest of which has a blind arcade, while the three others have each three lancets, the central arch alone in each being pierced for light. All have much dog-tooth. These towers were originally capped by lofty octagonal spires, which it is hoped may soon be restored. Even in their absence, however, the grace and harmony of the whole composition become more evident the longer it is studied.[g] The pinnacles now existing on the towers are late, and very poor.

New stone has been largely worked into the

[g] It may be well, however, to give here the very different opinion of a most competent critic :—" It is true that the west front of Ripon is pure E. E. in the sense of being nothing else ; but it is heavy, cold, bald, and unimaginative to excess. Of course it ought not to be judged without reference to the fact that, when built, it was a façade to a much narrower church. This would make it relatively better than it is now, though substantively just the same. All this is, however, purely matter of taste."—G. A. P.

whole front. The portals are almost entirely new, as
are the heads at the angles of the blind arcade in the
lower story.

IV. Leaving the rest of the exterior for the present, we
enter the Minster by the western door. Although the
view here must not be compared with that afforded by
the space and dignity of larger churches, it is neverthe-
less one of great interest, owing mainly to the unusual
width (87 feet) of the nave; for, eastward, the tall and
massive organ-screen shuts out the choir, the east
window of which is seen above it. Attention should
first be given to the two westernmost bays, those opening into the towers on either side, and the first bay of
the nave beyond.

The bays opening into the towers are Early English,
of the same date as the whole west front; but it is evident
that Archbishop Roger's work (seen in the first bay of
the nave beyond them, and in the transepts) materially
influenced their composition. Below, on either side,
is a lofty Early English arch, with many plain mouldings—(the capitals of the side piers, deeply undercut,
curiously resemble the Early English work in the
"Nine Altars" at Fountains). Above is a blind
arcade of four arches (the two in the centre higher
than the others), enclosed in a circular arch, with
plain rounded ribs. Above again, in the clerestory
stage, is a lofty circular arch, with a lower and sharply-
pointed one on each side. In this stage is a passage,
continued round the upper tier of lights in the west
window. The bays are divided by ringed shafts,

terminating in brackets, which should be compared with those of the same date at Fountains.

The double tier of lights in the west front is set off by clustered shafts, with much dog-tooth in the hollows. Seen from within, this front has a simple dignity effective in the highest degree.

The western towers (those at Lincoln and York may be compared) no doubt contained altars, though no record of their appropriation has been preserved. On three sides is a lofty pointed window (that toward the nave, closed before the restoration of 1862, has been opened and glazed). There is a staircase in the angles north and south-west.

V. The *nave* of Archbishop Roger's church had no aisles; and the piers of the existing nave rest on its foundations. The Early English western towers (Roger's nave seems to have had none) projected beyond it, and the present nave-aisles have been obtained by a line drawn from the outer angle of the towers to the central wall-pier of the transepts. The first bay beyond the towers preserves for us the character of Archbishop Roger's nave. The wall was plain in each bay below. Above was a triforium of two pointed arches, with a central detached shaft; and above again a clerestory of three narrow arches, that in the centre a little wider than the others. The effect must have been singularly grave and sombre, especially when the lights were filled with early stained glass.

A greater contrast than between this nave and that which now exists (Plate II.) can hardly be imagined. The

RIPON CATHEDRAL. THE NAVE

present nave of five bays was begun about 1502, and is unusually light and wide. The width of the central passage was determined by the width of Archbishop Roger's entire nave. The width of the nave and aisles (87 feet) is greater than that of any other English nave, York, Chichester (which has five aisles), Winchester, and St. Paul's excepted. Very graceful piers support a lofty clerestory. The brackets of the vaulting shafts are carried by angels bearing shields. The original panelled ceiling remained until 1829, when it was replaced by the present, with larger panels of a mahogany colour, which detract much from the beauty of the nave. The whole of this Perpendicular work would generally be supposed of much earlier date than is really the case.

The windows of the south aisle differ slightly from those of the north. The aisles were intended to have been groined, and the springers remain. The towers, which now form their west ends, projected, it must be remembered, beyond the earlier nave. This accounts for the windows on this side, and the various mouldings. At the east end of the nave are some remains of Archbishop Roger's nave, which will best be explained in connexion with the central tower.

There are few *monuments* of interest in the nave (or, indeed, in the cathedral). In the south aisle is a remarkable altar tomb, covered with a slab of grey marble, on which, in low relief, is the figure of a man in prayer, and near him that of a lion among trees. There is a defaced inscription below; but nothing is known of the history of the monument beyond a tradition that it is that of an Irish prince who died at Ripon on his return from Palestine, bringing with him

On a monument in the nave. Ripon.

a lion which had followed him like a dog. (This story is recorded of Roger de Mowbray, the famous crusader and the founder of Byland Abbey; and one very similar is the subject of the " Chevalier au Lion," one of the most favourite romances of the thirteenth century). The sculpture, as Mr. Walbran suggests, seems to represent some deliverance from a lion. Its date is uncertain. In the westernmost bay of the same aisle is the Perpendicular font, and by its side that which was provided when Archbishop Roger erected the nave. It is circular and massive, without stem or base, and is ornamented by an arcade with round trefoiled heads.

Some fourteenth century *stained glass*, of great excellence, remained until the present restoration in the westernmost window of the south aisle, to which it had been removed from the east window of the choir.

These fragments are roundels, representing St. Peter, St. Paul, and St. Andrew, and some other saints not easily distinguished. They have been removed into the library; and the window in which they were placed is now filled with modern glass. There is some modern glass (of various quality) in other windows of the aisles.

VI. The crypt is entered from the south-east bay of the nave; but the whole of the upper church may first be examined. The *central tower* (part of Archbishop Roger's work) had become ruinous in 1459; when the south and east sides were rebuilt as we now see them. The original arrangement remains north and west; but these arches, if the chapter funds had permitted, would probably have been altered like the others. At present the great mass of Perpendicular masonry at the south-west angle projects awkwardly enough. It will be seen that the original arches were higher north and south than east and west, and that the north wall of the tower overhangs to an almost startling extent; an intentional, though very bold arrangement, rendered necessary perhaps by the fact that the ancient crypt extends below the tower, and so made it impossible to bring the north walls of nave and choir into straight line. The arrangement above the main tower arches should be noticed (the small openings in the wall between the pointed lights of the clerestory are no part of the original design, but were produced by walling up spaces, probably in the seventeenth century, with an idea of strengthening the tower, which was severely rent

on the north side).   On both sides of the nave, adjoining the western arch, portions of Archbishop Roger's
nave remain; on the north side part of the vaulting
shaft, and one bay of the triforium; on the south the
triforium remains, but closed up.   These portions
resemble the more complete bay at the west end.
Against the wall (north) is the monument, with bust,
of Hugh Ripley, last "Wakeman" (as the chief officer
of the town was anciently called, from his rule of the
"wake" or watch) and first "Mayor" of Ripon, died
1637.   On the inner side of the north-west tower-arch
a figure of James I. (in whose time Ripon was incorporated, and the Wakeman became a Mayor) is placed
on a semi-detached shaft.   The British Solomon has
probably dethroned St. Wilfrid.   The statue was
brought from York Minster, where it long occupied
a niche in the choir screen.

VII. The *transepts* retain Archbishop Roger's work
more entirely than any other portion of the church.
The north transept especially is almost unchanged.
Each transept has an eastern aisle of two bays.

The north transept had originally on its west side
two round-headed windows in its lower story, one of
which remains.   The other was cut through when the
Perpendicular arch was · formed, opening from the
nave aisle.   The triforium has two broad arches in
each bay, with a central detached shaft. The clerestory
above has three arches in each bay; that in the centre
round, the others pointed.   Triple vaulting shafts,
with cushioned capitals (modern, and grafted on the

old shafts), divide the bays. The arrangement of the north end of the transept is the same, except that the bays are more compressed. (The manner in which this is effected in the clerestory is especially noticeable.) The piers of the eastern aisle have square abaci. The arches are narrow, lofty, and sharply pointed. Within the aisle the capitals of the shafts are leafed, and at the bases of the windows are brackets with heads. Running under the east windows of this aisle, and along the north end, are traces of a painted, intersected arcade. (For the doorway in this transept, especially characteristic on the exterior. See § xv.)

The whole of this work greatly resembles, in its general character, the remains of Archbishop Roger's palace at York, particularly the building now used as the Chapter Library, and which was probably the chapel of his palace. A portion of the choir of the monastic church at Whitby (south side), is similar in composition. It has been suggested that the design is rather Continental than English; and this was certainly the case with the very peculiar nave. The transepts at Fountains should be compared. They are nearly of the same date; but the Early English is hardly developed at all in them, whilst at Ripon its influence is more evident than that of the passing-away Norman.

The groining of the transept is a miserable work of papier maché, which must surely be soon removed. Outside the aisle is the much-shattered monument, with effigies, of Sir Thomas Markenfield and wife (died

1497). The chantry of St. Andrew, within the aisle, was
the burial-place of the Markenfields, a family resident
for many centuries at Markenfield Hall, near Ripon,
till, in 1569, Thomas Markenfield took an active part
in the rising of the North, and on his attainder his
estates were forfeited to the Crown. In it is the altar-
tomb of another Sir Thomas Markenfield (living temp.
Richard II., and aged thirty-nine when he was a
witness in the Scrope and Grosvenor case), whose
armour deserves notice. The sword-sheath is richly
decorated. His livery collar represents the pales of a
park, and the badge suspended from it is a couchant
stag, surrounded by similar pales. The same paling
surrounds his helmet, in front of which are the letters
I H C. Close by is the monument of Sir Edward
Blackett of Newby (died 1718), who reposes thereon
in a Ramillies wig and laced waistcoat, attended by
two wives. The helmets, gloves, and achievements
here were used at his funeral.

The transept windows are filled with modern stained
glass, which calls for no especial notice.

The *south transept* has precisely resembled the
north; but the eastern aisle was altered at the same
time (probably) as the central tower. Archbishop
Roger's shafts remain against the east wall; but the
entire front of the aisle (including triforium and clerestory) is Perpendicular; although the original vaulting-
shafts remain between the bays, and the Perpendicular
work is grouped with them.

Against the south wall of the transept is a copy of

the Choragic Monument of Lysicrates at Athens, a memorial of William Weddell, of Newby, "in whom every virtue that ennobles the human mind was united with every elegance that adorns it." The monument is "a faint emblem of his refined taste;" but to those whose minds are less elegantly adorned it will appear singularly out of place. The bust is by Nollekens.

In the aisle is a tablet for Sir John Mallorie, of Studley, who defended Skipton Castle for Charles I.; and another for the Aislabies, also lords of Studley. At the north-east corner of the aisle steps lead upward to the library (see § XIII.). The position of these steps has been somewhat altered during the restoration; and (1866) fresco paintings were discovered on the slope of the head of the Transition Norman window, through which the entrance was formed to the library ('Christ coming to Judgment'), and on the north wall of the aisle ('The Wise Men's Offerings).

VIII. The *Choir Screen*, Perpendicular, like the piers between which it rises, was, like them, completed soon after 1459. It is a mass of rich tabernacle work, 19 feet high, with four niches on either side of the door, and a range of smaller ones above. Over the door is a representation of the Holy Father with censing angels. A small figure of the Saviour in the lap of the Father has been removed. In the moulding above the tabernacle work is a long row of shields with rests. These are tiles. One alone has a bearing, that of Kendal of Ripon. The doors are of the same date as the screen. Among the shields on them are those

M

of the see of York, St. William of York, and St. Wilfrid
(three stars). The *organ*, by Booth, of Leeds (but
retaining the choir organ of Father Schmidt, built on
the spot in 1695), was erected in 1833.

IX. Through the screen we enter the *Choir* (Plate III.),
which, including (as it now does) the Presbytery, contains work of three distinct periods, Transition Norman,
Decorated, and Perpendicular. The three westernmost
bays on the north side, and on the south the second
pier from the east, are Archbishop Roger's work; and
the existing choir with its aisles is built (probably) on
the foundations of his choir. The three bays opposite
(south side) are Perpendicular, built after the ruin of
the central tower in 1459; and the two eastern bays,
or presbytery, are Early Decorated (1288-1300). Archbishop Roger's work resembles that in the transepts; but
the fine group of vaulting-shafts should be especially
noticed. The clustered piers have square abaci, with
remarkable protruding square brackets, on which some
of these vaulting-shafts rest. The triforium is glazed
like the clerestory; but this change took place in the
Perpendicular period. The arches of the triforium opened
originally into the roof space above the vaulting of the
aisles. This roof was lowered after 1459, and the
triforium opening filled with glass. " Uninformed of
this fact, the student has often gazed in astonishment
on the two pointed lights of the round-headed arch,
divided by a slender column, and ornamented with
those sharp cusps, which are, in reality, shown from
the more modern mullion behind."—*J. R. Walbran.*

RIPON CATHEDRAL. THE CHOIR.

The decorated work of the two eastern bays has a certain retrospective character, designed to assimilate it in some degree with the Transition-Norman west of it. The triforium openings (now lights) are enclosed, like Archbishop Roger's, in a circular arch. The clerestory passage has a double plane of tracery. On the south side the junction of the Decorated and Perpendicular is marked by two monastic heads at the spring of the main arch. Opposite, north, are two smaller heads. The leafage of the Decorated portion (executed at the time when natural foliage was copied with the utmost care and accuracy) is very beautiful, and deserves special notice. The great east window, of seven lights, is unusually fine. At the angles are shafts with capitals of leafage; brackets support an inner rib, running round the soffete. The glass, which now fills the window, is by Wailes, of Newcastle, and was placed there in 1854, in commemoration of the erection of the see of Ripon in 1836. It cost 1000*l.*, but is not too good. The original Decorated trefoiled arcade, like that in the aisles of the Presbytery, has been restored, below the east window, by Mr. Scott.

The three westernmost bays on the south side of the choir are Perpendicular; but the triforium still retains the circular arch. The wall space below is panelled.

The wooden roof of the choir is modern. The lath-and-plaster groining, erected in 1829, has been removed under Mr. Scott's direction, and a wooden vaulting substituted, of the same pitch, plan, and section of ribs as the Decorated vault, which had been also of wood. This was proved by comparison of the section of the vaulting ribs with the similar indications in the wooden bosses or centre knobs which had been preserved after the fall of the spire in 1660, when the original Decorated vault was broken through. Nearly all these bosses were replaced in the groining of 1829, and, after proper cleaning, are fixed in the present vault. They represent, beginning from the east,—an unknown head, the Good Samaritan, the expulsion from Paradise, the Virgin with vase of lilies, the Crucifixion (modern), and a King and Bishop seated. The oak vaulting is relieved with patterns in colour, and on the ribs are fillets of gilding. On the south side of the altar are three sedilia, late Perpendicular in character, but showing small heads and details worth attention.

The choir retains much of its ancient *wood-work.* That at the west end shows a good mass of tabernacle-work, with angels bearing shields at the terminations of the lower canopies. This is of the fifteenth century, as are the carved subsellia throughout the stalls, on which are the dates 1489 and 1494. The finials of the stalls are especially fine. In front of the bishop's stall is an elephant with a "castle" on his back, in which are fighting men,—one throwing a stone, another behind with a horn. The finial of the opposite stall, on the north side, has a very grotesque monkey. The subsellia are good and well carved.

RIPON CATHEDRAL. NORTH AISLE OF CHOIR

The spies with grapes, Sampson with the gates of Gaza, a fox preaching to geese, and a griffin among rabbits, one of which has been seized, whilst the rest are escaping into their holes—are especially notice-able. All this wood-work has been most carefully and judiciously restored, under the direction of Mr. G. G. Scott. Some portions, above the eastern stalls, which had been "renewed" in the seventeenth century, have been removed altogether, and replaced by cano-pies in accordance with the original design. An Episcopal throne, erected in 1812, has been taken down; and the bishop now occupies the easternmost stall on the south side, which appears (from the sculp-ture of a mitre on the back) to have been that origin-ally assigned to the Archbishop of York. The opposite stall was occupied by the Wakeman of Ripon. At the east end of both of these stalls is a small pierced quatrefoil, with a sliding cover of wood. These openings afforded a view of the high altar to the occupiers of the stalls.

The screen work which encloses the choir is of the fifteenth century, and of the usual Yorkshire type, in accordance with which the upper part of the heading alone is filled with tracery.

X. The *north choir aisle* (Plate IV.) follows the architecture of the choir, having its three westernmost bays Transition (Archbishop Roger's), and the two eastern, Decorated. The western bays have broad lancet windows (more resembling Early French than Early English), with Perpendicular tracery inserted.

(The windows are perhaps altogether insertions of the Decorated period.) The vaulting is quadripartite. A Decorated window, with an arcade below it, terminates the aisle.

XI. The *shrine of St. Wilfrid* rested, it is supposed, in this easternmost bay of the north aisle. Leland, in his Itinerary, asserts that the saint's " reliquiæ " were buried " on the north side of the Quiere," " sub arcu prope mag. altare." On the other hand, Odo, Archbishop of Canterbury, in his preface to ' Frithgode's Metrical Life of Wilfrid,' asserts that on visiting the old monastery here he found the grave of Wilfrid in a state of utter neglect, and removed his bones to Canterbury.[h] It is certain, on the one hand, that the canons of Ripon asserted that they had possession of St. Wilfrid's relics, and that pilgrimages were made to his shrine here from an early period (the banner of St. Wilfrid, which stood over his tomb, was one of the three displayed at the battle of the Standard in 1138. The others were the banners of St. Peter of York and St. John of Beverley);—and, on the other hand, that Gervase of Canterbury, writing after the rebuilding of the cathedral there by William of Sens at the end of the twelfth century, asserts that the body of St. Wilfrid of York reposed in the eastern chapel of the cathedral, which was burnt in 1174, and that it was removed, with the relics of other saints, into the new church. It would seem most probable that the Canterbury story (supported by Archbishop Odo's positive

[h] Mabillon, Act. Ord. Bened., § 5, p. 283.

assertion) is the true one; although the canons of
Ripon may have honestly believed that they possessed
their patron's body. The discordant assertions may
be reconciled in a certain degree by a statement of
Eadmer, who, in his Life of Wilfrid, written in the
twelfth century, after informing us that Wilfrid's body
was removed to Canterbury by Archbishop Odo, says
that, from respect to the place which Wilfrid had
loved beyond all others in his lifetime, a small portion
of his remains was left at Ripon, and deposited in a
suitable place.[l] The remains, whatever they may have
been, were translated by Archbishop Walter Gray, and
placed in a fitting shrine.[k]

XII. The *south* aisle resembles that opposite. The
windows of Archbishop Roger's portion are placed
high in the wall, on account of the Norman chapter-
house and vestry, which abut the aisle. They now
look into the Lady Loft. (see § XIII.) Vaulting-shafts
rise between the windows. They are carried on very
remarkable and unusual corbels, of singularly classical
character, and, so far as is known, peculiar to this
work of Roger's at Ripon. The position of one of

---

[l] "Ne tamen locus quem ipse beatus Wilfridus, dum in corpore
degeret, præ ceteris amavit, ipsius reliquiis penitus privaretur,
aliquantula earum pars ab eis est cum pulvere tenta, atque in
loco convenienti reposita."—*Cott. M.S. Calig.* A 8, fol. 80 *b.*

[k]   "Wilfridi reliquias de theca levavit,
          In capsam argenteam digne collucavit."

From the Metrical History of the Archbishops in MSS. Cotton.
Cleopatra. C. iv. Quoted in Raine's 'Archbishops of York,' i.
p. 292.

these brackets in the north choir aisle is shown in
Plate IV.

Bracket in South Choir Aisle, Ripon.

In the bay adjoining the vestry-door is a long, square
lavatory; and the piscina of the chapel in the eastern
bay remains. Staircases ascend into the buttress
turrets at the exterior angle of both aisles (see *post—
Exterior*).

XIII. The *chapter-house* is entered from the second
bay of the south aisle (counting from the west). This,
with the vestry eastward of it, was either, as Mr.
Walbran has suggested, built over the aisle, or, as
other archæologists suppose, the choir, of a Norman
church, the work of Archbishop Thomas of Bayeux
(1070—1100), after the devastation of Yorkshire by
the Conqueror in 1069. The crypt below represents
this church, and is of Norman date. The rest of the

church was most likely destroyed by Archbishop Roger, who converted this remaining portion into a chapter-house and sacristy for his new minster. The vaulting and two central piers of the chapter-house are Early English, of later date than Archbishop Roger's work, but the walls and circular windows are of his time. The north wall shows portions of a Norman arcade, indicating apparently that this wall, like the crypt, was retained when the rest of the church was pulled down.[1] At the north-west angle a doorway opens to a flight of steps leading to the crypt. (See *post*, § XVII.)

The *Vestry* or sacristy, east of the chapter-house, is of the same character. Foundations of the choir buttresses (circ. 1288) project into it on the north side; but the Norman arcade is more evident here than in the chapter-house. The east end is apsidal, with the base of the altar remaining. On the south side is a small lateral apse, forming a room for storing treasures of the church. In it is a piscina or lavatory.

Above both chapter-house and vestry, and approached by steps from the south transept, is the *Lady Loft*, a chapel of Decorated date (circ. 1330), which formed the ancient Lady Chapel of the Minster, and now serves as the chapter library. There are no books here calling for special attention.

XIV. Returning to the nave, we enter, by stairs at its north-east angle, the *crypt*, called " *St. Wilfrid's*

---

[1] See *post*, Appendix to Part I.

Needle" (Plate V.), in many respects the most interesting portion of the whole church. A long and narrow passage leads to a cell, cylindrically vaulted, 7 feet 9 inches

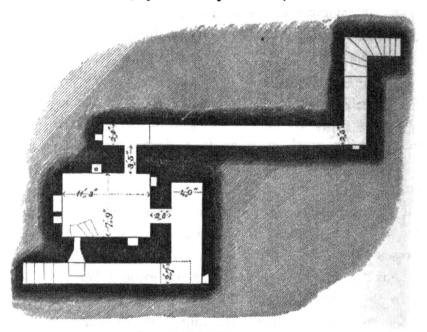

Plan of St. Wilfrid's Crypt.

wide, 11 feet 3 inches long, and 9 feet 4 inches high; in each wall are plain niches, with semicircular heads. One of these (west) has a deep basin in the base; and others, apertures at the back, as if for the smoke of a lamp. The larger niche at the east end (see the Plate,) may perhaps have contained a crucifix. At the northeast angle is the opening called St. Wilfrid's Needle, (marked in the plan by its funnel-shaped mouth, leading to the further passage; and in Plate V. by the letter *a*), which is said by Camden to have been used as an ordeal for women accused of unchastity. If they could

PLATE V.

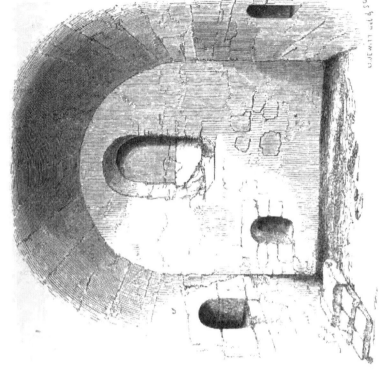

ST. WILFRID'S NEEDLE.
(a) THE NEEDLE.

PASSAGE, SHOWING THE EXTERIOR OF
'THE NEEDLE'.

not pass through it they were considered guilty.[m] At
the west end a doorway opens into another passage,
4 ft. in breadth; and turning at right angles into one
much narrower. This latter passage runs parallel with
the north side of the main crypt. The pierced niche
called the "Needle," opens into it; and at its eastern
end are rude steps which may perhaps have once
ascended to the upper church. It is possible that other
cells may exist, although they have yet to be discovered.
(The crypt itself is untouched; but whether the passages
were to any extent altered on the construction of
Archbishop Roger's church, or at a later period, is not
altogether certain. The western portion of the passage
leading from the nave has an early sepulchral stone in
the roof, proving that some change has taken place
there at any rate.) The strongly marked Roman
character of this crypt will at once strike the visitor.
It has, indeed, been regarded by some antiquaries as a
Roman sepulchre; but a crypt of very similar character exists at Hexham, in Northumberland, beneath
the conventual church, which Wilfrid founded there;

---

[m] This use of the opening (if in truth such an use was ever
made of it) represents a very ancient piece of superstition. A
passage in broken rock on the side of Rhosbery Topping, in the
North Riding was also called "St. Wilfrid's Needle," and some
benefit was thought to follow from creeping through it. In
Cornwall, creeping through the "Holed Stone" (Men-an-tol) on
the Lanyon Downs, cures the "crick." A touchstone resembling
the ordeal of the needle existed in the church of Boxley in Kent,
in the shape of a small figure of St. Rumbald, which only those
could lift who had never sinned in thought or in deed.

and it is, therefore, reasonable to conclude that this is of the same date, and that it marks the site, not of Wilfrid's monastic church here, which, it is known, stood elsewhere,[n] but of a second church, either founded by him, or constructed by the same workmen.[o] It is, therefore, the most perfect existing relic of the first age of Christianity in Yorkshire, and as such cannot but be regarded with the utmost interest and veneration. The crypts, both here and at Hexham, are popularly known as " confessionals ; " but it is more probable that they were used for the exhibition

[n] "The old Abbay of Ripon stode wher now is a chapelle of our Lady, in a Botom one close distant by [200 yards] from the new Minstre."—Leland, *Itin.*, vol. i. p. 92.   This was the " Old Abbay" (Wilfrid's Basilica) destroyed by Eadred. *See* § 1. " When any excavation is made on the site of Wilfrid's Monastery (at Ripon), a number of small white tesseræ are discovered, such as are only found in this country in or near Roman camps.   In the Chapel of St. Mary Magdalene, close to Ripon, before the altar, lies a coloured tesselated pavement, which cannot but be traced to the same source, and which has evidently been constructed to fill a position such as it at present occupies."—*Architecture of Hexham Priory*, in Raine's Hexham, vol. ii., p. xxviii. Wilfrid is known to have imported a number of Gallic and Italian workmen, and it is probable that both tesseræ and pavement are relics of their handiwork.

[o] May not this church have been founded by Eadhed, who in the year 678 became Bishop of Ripon? (See Part II.) Although Wilfrid was not then present at Ripon, his monastery was undisturbed, and it is not very probable that the monks would have received Eadhed, whom they would regard as an intruder. Hence he may have been induced to found another church to serve as his cathedral,—using the plans and workmen which Wilfrid had introduced.

of relics at certain periods, "according to an ancient custom still in use on the Continent; the faithful descend by one staircase, pass along the narrow passage, look through the opening in the wall at the relics, and then pass on, ascending by the other staircase."— *J. H. Parker.* They belong, however, to a period so remote, and are connected with local rituals and observances so little known to us, that it is impossible to ascertain their original purpose with certainty.[p] It is an important fact which has not been previously noticed in describing or speculating on the original purposes of these crypts, that there is a "needle" or voided niche at Hexham, as well as at Ripon, and in the same position in the north wall; but in the former instance it has not been enlarged on the side toward the passage, as in the latter case.

XV. Passing once more to the *exterior* of the church, the visitor should remark the good double-headed Perpendicular buttresses of the nave. The elevation of the *north* transept is the most perfect remaining example of Archbishop Roger's work. Its flanking buttresses retain their original turret capping, pierced at the summit by two round-headed openings, divided by a plain mullion,—"a good example of an arrange-

[p] An excellent notice of the Ripon crypt by Mr. Walbran will be found in the York vol. of the 'Archæological Institute,' and another, by the same writer, on the crypt of Hexham, in his account of the fabric of that church embodied in Raine's 'Priory of Hexham,' vol. ii. (Surtees Society.) An extract from this latter account, in which the two crypts are compared will be found in the Appendix (A) to Part I.

ment, which shows the germ of a spire and pinnacles "
—(*J. R. Walbran*),—and recalling early work at Kirk-
stall Abbey.   The shafts at the angles of the windows,
and the doorway (Plate VI.), with trefoiled heading,
and side shafts with foliated capitals (Plate VII.),
should be noticed.   This doorway exemplifies the peculiar character of Roger's work better perhaps than any
other part of the cathedral.   The capitals, very graceful,
and almost Corinthian in detail, are especially note-
worthy.   Above the eastern aisle of the transept was
(as at Canterbury, before the fire of 1174, at Gloucester, and in other great Norman churches), a chapel,
which was destroyed when the triforium was altered
throughout the choir.   The roof was then settled to
the present aisle.   Archbishop Roger's base moulding
should be remarked, running round the transept and
part of the choir.

   At the east end of the church the massive Decorated
buttresses between the choir and aisles form the most
striking feature.   The windows, with their rich foliations, are very fine examples of early Decorated, and the
whole composition (see Plate IX. *post*) is finely conceived.   The window in the gable (above the east
window) lights the space between the choir-vaulting
and the roof.   In the pinnacle of the south-east buttress
is a remarkable place of concealment, or perhaps of imprisonment.   (Every religious house had its "laterna,"
or prison for refractory members.   Sometimes, as at
Fountains, there were several, of different degrees of
severity.)   On getting to the head of the stairs, which

NORTH DOOR.　RIPON CATHEDRAL.

CAPITALS OF THE NORTH DOOR. RIPON CATHEDRAL

THE CHAPTER HOUSE AND EARLY NORMAN CHURCH
RIPON CATHEDRAL

wind up the buttress, no opening is seen; but when
what appears to be the roof is pushed against, a trap
door opens, through which the prisoner might be thrust
into his narrow quarters.   By the side of the staircase
turret is a garderobe seat, inserted within the battlement of the roof of the Lady Loft.

XVI. In the vestry and chapter-house (Plate VIII.),
remark the Norman string-course (Archbishop Roger's
work) which runs round between the earlier building
and the Lady Loft.   This latter is distinguished by its
square-headed windows, the tracery of which is formed
by intersecting arches.   Under both the vestry and
chapter-house is a crypt, no doubt of Norman date.
Owing to the fall of the ground, a range of round-
headed windows has been obtained for the crypt, giving,
by the double tier of Norman lights, (the second tier,
in the chapter-house, is of Archbishop Roger's time,) a
peculiar character to the whole elevation.   (In Plate
VIII. these double lights are seen.)   The western
portion of the crypt is walled off, and used for interment.   The eastern, until 1866, formed what was
known as the bone-house, and was filled with an array
of human relics resembling the ossuaries attached to
most village churches in Brittany.   Bones and skulls
were piled up in vast numbers on its north side;
and for 3 feet beneath the surface of the ground the
crumbling dust was that of the ancient inhabitants of
Ripon.   All these remains have been removed and
buried.   The vault of the crypt is supported by
square pillars, with plain capitals.   These have been

strengthened at a later period, as have the semi-circular vaulting arches themselves—no doubt at the time when the chapter-house was vaulted, and additional pressure was introduced. The windows have a double splay, outward and inward. This has been thought to mark a Saxon building, but the piers are plainly of Norman date.[q] Over the door of the bone-house is the head of a cross which may very well be Saxon. It was found in 1832, in taking down a wall (temp. Henry .VIII.) at the east end of the choir.

Some thirteenth century sepulchral slabs are collected under the east window. Near the south transept is a tombstone with a curious epitaph for six infants.

The cathedral is so closely surrounded with buildings that it is difficult to obtain a good view. That, however, from the churchyard, on the south-east side, is striking and picturesque (Plate IX.). It embraces also the oldest portions of the church, besides much of the later additions. It is to be regretted that the churchyard is closed to the public; so that this, by far the best view of the cathedral, is not always to be studied at leisure. At a distance, and from the low hills about Ripon, the church rises finely above the city, and is a conspicuous mark from the hills which border the great plain of York.

[q] See the Appendix (B) to Part I.

PLATE IX.

RIPON CATHEDRAL.

J. JEWITT. del & sc.

RIPON CATHEDRAL. SOUTH-EAST VIEW

APPENDIX (A) TO PART I.

§ XIV.

"BOTH Eddi and Prior Richard seem to have been especially struck with the apartments which Wilfrid constructed deep down below this church" [at Hexham], "and it may have been that he first introduced such features in English churches. Eddi, speaking of the church, says:—'cujus profunditatem in terra cum domibus mirifice politis lapidibus fundatam,' &c. Richard speaks more explicitly of crypts, underground oratories, and winding passages. Of these, with their appurtenant passages, only one is now known, and that so recently discovered as the year 1726, although most probably it will be found at a future day to communicate with another. Whatever position it may have occupied with reference to its original superstructure, it was left by the Early English rebuilders' [of the Priory Church] 'at the eastern extremity of their nave. That portion of the church (the nave) is now destroyed, and the crypt is therefore now entered from the churchyard. There is no object of similar character in the kingdom, except one in the cathedral church of Ripon, which unquestionably owes its origin to St. Wilfrid. . . . . . The chapel of the crypt at Hexham is rather larger than that of Ripon, measuring 13 feet 4 inches, by 8 feet, against 11 feet 3 inches, by 7 feet 9 inches. It is also placed much deeper in the ground, and is constructed almost entirely of stones brought from a Roman building, whereas the other is formed of the grit-stone of the country. In the one, the cells at the west end of the flanking passages have triangular roofs; in the other, the cells are not defined from the passages by arches, and are covered with flat stones. At Hexham the anti-chapel has a barrel-vault, at Ripon a semi-vault only. In the one, two passages lead eastward, and one southward; the other has but one outlet towards the choir. In this crypt the heads of the niches are flat, and there are none in the eastern wall; in the other they have semi-circular heads; and there is one on the north side of the space once occupied by the altar, and a larger one above that space in the middle of the wall. But both the crypts have obviously proceeded from a common type, although the idea is more elaborated at Hexham than at Ripon. Both chapels have their entrances in the same positions. In both, the semi-circular heads of the doorways, which are of the same height—6 feet 3 inches—are cut out of horizontal slabs. The passages in each agree in width within an inch. Both have funnel-like apertures in the heads of the niches, and deep round basins in the bases. In both, the north-east niche is pierced through to the passage behind. Both have a small rectangular opening in the roof of the anti-chapel, which may have been connected by a flue with the floor of the church above; and both have been plastered throughout.

" Irrespective of the general interest which must attach to this crypt as one of the earliest and most curious of the Saxon structures that we possess, it is remarkable from having been built almost entirely of stones which have been used in an earlier work. Two of these bear Roman inscriptions, and the rest are presumed to have had the same origin. Evidently they have been used here as the most eligible materials which Wilfrid could command, and, as is shown by their positions, not for the sake of ornament or enriching the character of his design."—' Raine's Priory of Hexham,' vol. ii., pp. xxxv., xxxvi., xxxvii. This account of the fabric of the Priory was contributed by J. R. Walbran, Esq.

APPENDIX (B.)

§ XVI.

THE architectural history and dates of the chapter-house and sacristy, with the crypt beneath them, are by no means easily read. It seems tolerably certain, however, that the crypt, with the wall between it and the choir, belong to the Norman (the windows of the crypt, with double splay, are of Early character) church of Archbishop Thomas (1070-1100); that the vaulting of this crypt was plain, having only transverse arches of square section, supported on square piers of masonry; and that it terminated in an apse. These transverse arches and piers still remain. Archbishop Roger took down this old church, only retaining the north wall and the crypt; above which he built his chapter-house. (The circular windows are of this date.) But he also seems to have taken down the apse of the crypt, and to have rebuilt it from the ground, finishing the whole with a stone roof; and apparently considering that the crypt was not strong enough to carry the new building, he added the transverse vaulting ribs, and the pillars which carry them. The manner in which the transverse vaulting ribs have been let into the older square piers seems to prove this with sufficient clearness. The apse has on the exterior Roger's base, of perfectly Early English character, and contains a trefoil-headed window. In the fourteenth century the stone roof of Roger's chapter-house was taken off, and the present Lady Loft was carried up.

Thus much would appear tolerably certain. But whether the crypt was below the choir of the first Norman church, or under the north aisle, is matter for discussion. Those who think that it represents the choir, insist on the extreme improbability that any other portion of the church would have been so underbuilt. But, on the other hand, if it were under the choir, in what part of the church was the Saxon crypt included? It certainly would have been *within* the Norman church, if it did not influence its site and plan, as we know it did with the church of Archbishop Roger. The plan also of the church at Hexham is distinctly influenced by the Saxon crypt.

To add to the difficulties, it has been also suggested that the Norman arcade against the north wall of the chapter-house is really built against the exterior face of Roger's south choir aisle; the proof being a string-course in the latter work, partly cut away when the former was erected to support the vaulting. If this be so, it would follow that when Roger built the choir the present chapter-house and vestry were either in ruins, or that he intended to remove them.

RIPON CATHEDRAL.

———◆◆———

PART II.

The Monastery and the See.

THE earliest mention of Ripon occurs in the 'Ecclesiastical History' of Bede, who tells us that Alchfrid of Northumbria gave to the famous Wilfrid a certain monastery "in the place which is called Inhrypum," which a short time before he had given to the Scottish religious at Melrose.[a] The monks of Melrose had founded the monastery at Ripon, and Cuthbert, the future saint of Lindisfarne and Durham (see 'Durham Cathedral,' Pt. II.), had there filled the office of "præpositus hospitum," or "hostiller," whose duty it was to receive and provide for strangers.[b] After the Council of Whitby in 664, which established the Roman usages in opposition to those of the Irish Scots, Colman, the Scottish Bishop of Lindisfarne, resigned his see;

---

[a] Porro Alchfrid magistrum habens eruditionis Christianæ Vilfridum virum doctissimum . . . . hujus doctrinam omnibus Scottorum traditionibus jure præferendam sciebat; unde ei etiam donaverat monasterium quadraginta familiarum in loco qui dicitur Inhrypum, quem videlicet locum paulo ante eis qui Scottos sequebantur, in possessionem monasterii dederat. Sed quia illi postmodum, data sibi optione, magis loco cedere quam suam mutare consuetudinem, volebant, dedit eum illi, qui dignam loco et doctrinam haberet, et vitam. Beda, H. E., L. iii. c. 25.

[b] Beda, V. S. Cuthberti.

and the monks of Ripon, who of course were Scots, left their newly-planted colony and returned to Melrose. It was either in the same year or very soon afterwards that the abandoned monastery was granted to Wilfrid.

It is traditionally asserted that Wilfrid was born in the neighbourhood of Ripon, and his parents are said to have been noble. At a very early age he proceeded to the court of the Northumbrian Queen Eanfleda, who sent him to the monastery of Lindisfarne. Thence, after some years, still assisted by Eanfleda, he went to Erconbert, King of Kent, and in 652 left England on a pilgrimage to Rome. He was absent five years; partly at Rome, and partly at Lyons. At Lyons he received the tonsure after the Roman fashion, from (it is said) the prelate Dalfinus; and, at any rate, he returned to England fervently attached to Roman usages in opposition to those of the Scots, in which he had been instructed at Lindisfarne. Alchfrid was at this time ruler of Deira under his father Oswi. He too had become a follower of Rome, and under his auspices the synod was held at Whitby, at which Wilfrid appeared as the great champion of Rome, and which decided in his favour. Wilfrid then seems to have succeeded the Scots in their monastery at Ripon. He had already been ordained priest.

On the death of Tuda, the successor of Colman, Wilfrid was persuaded to accept the northern bishopric. He went (664) to France to receive consecration at the hands of Agilbert, once Bishop of the West Saxons, and at that time of Paris; was shipwrecked on the coast of Sussex on his return, and then found that Oswi of Northumbria had returned to the Scottish teaching, and had placed Ceadda in the northern see. (See 'York Cathedral,' Pt. II.) Wilfrid retired to Ripon, but in 669 became Bishop of Northumbria on Ceadda's resignation. (See 'York,' Pt. II.) Wilfrid abandoned the see in 678. The history of his subsequent wanderings need not be told here. He became at last Bishop of Hexham, and died October 12, 709, in the monastery of Oundle, which he had himself established. At his own request his body was conveyed to Ripon for interment.

At Ripon, Wilfrid, soon after his establishment in the see of York in 669, rebuilt the church and monastery a few yards west of the site of the old Scottish church. "The only account of the church left us by Eddi, who resided and ministered within its walls, is that it was a 'basilica' constructed of wrought stones from the foundation, and that divers pillars and porticoes entered into its arrangement. The employment of stone instead of the usual materials of wood and thatch is a proof of the unusual character of the building; and the allusion to pillars and porticoes suggests the plan of a structure with side-aisles, and not improbably a transept; a partial copy, perhaps, of some basilica which had engaged his preference in France or Italy, if there were no structures left by the Romans in Britain, and even in his own own diocese, which he was content to copy."[d] The dedication of this church to St. Peter was celebrated with unusual magnificence. The Kings Egfrid and Ælwin were present, and the feast which followed the dedication lasted for three days and three nights. In all probability (see Pt. I., §§ i., xiv.), either Wilfrid or Bishop Eadhead built a second church at Ripon on the site of the existing Cathedral. At any rate the basilica which Eddius describes was, as Leland tells us, at some little distance from the Cathedral (see Pt. I., § xiv. note), and was destroyed by Eadred in 948.

Among the monks of Ripon were Willebrord, the apostle of Friesland, who was educated here under Wilfrid, and

[d] 'St. Wilfrid and the Saxon Church of Ripon.' By J. R. Walbran. Yorkshire Architectural Society. Vol. V. Part I., p. 63.

Stephen Eddi or Eddius, the biographer and chaplain of Wilfrid. Wilfrid's monks were most probably Benedictines. A body of Augustinian Canons was in possession at the time of the Domesday Survey, and remained attached to the church until the dissolution (see Pt. I., § i.).

In the year 678, after Archbishop Theodore had divided the Northumbrian diocese into the four bishoprics of York, Lindisfarne, Hexham, and Witherne (see 'York,' Pt. II., *Wilfrid*), he made (apparently after the abandonment of his see by Wilfrid) a further change by appointing EADHED, who had returned from the newly-erected see of Lindisse or Sidnacester, to a diocese of which the see was fixed at Ripon. "We have no information as to the extent of country placed under his jurisdiction, but as the limits of the see of York bounded it on the east, it is probable that much of the same district was assigned as that which now constitutes the second Bishopric of Ripon."[*] Little is recorded of Eadhed, and the time of his death or resignation is unknown. He had no successor; and the see of Ripon remained in abeyance for more than a thousand years, until, in 1836, in consequence of the Report of the Ecclesiastical Commissioners, it was re-erected. The diocese now includes "that part of the county of York heretofore in the diocese of Chester, the deanery of Craven, and such parts of the deanery of the Ainsty and Pontefract, in the county and diocese of York, as lie to the westward of the liberty of the Ainsty and the wapentakes of Barkstone Ash, Osgoldcross, and Staincross—a district containing the great towns of Leeds, Bradford, Halifax, Wakefield, and Huddersfield."

The Bishops of Ripon, since this restoration of the see, have been—

[A.D. 1836, translated to Durham 1856.] CHARLES THOMAS LONGLEY.

[A.D. 1857.] ROBERT BICKERSTETH.

[*] J. R. Walbran, ut sup.

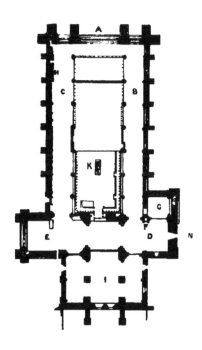

REFERENCES.

A *East Window.*
B *South Aisle of Choir.*
C *North Aisle of Choir.*
D *South Transept.*
E *North Transept.*
F *Ancient Well.*

G *St. Catherine's Chapel.*
H *Monumental Recesses.*
I *Nave: now Parish Church.*
K *Bross of Bishop Bell.*
M *Monument of Prior Senhouse.*
N *Present entrance Portal.*

PLAN OF CARLISLE CATHEDRAL.

Scale 100 feet to 1 inch.

CARLISLE CATHEDRAL.

MONUMENTAL RECESSES, IN THE NORTH AISLE.

DECORATED WINDOW. EAST END. CARLISLE CATHEDRAL.

CARLISLE CATHEDRAL.

———◦✦◦———

PART I.

History and Details.

I. CARLISLE, the British Caer Luel (Caer-Luelid of
Nennius), the Roman Lugubalia, was occupied by the
Anglians of Northumbria after their conquest of the
British kingdom of Cumbria; and at least one religious house had been established in the city before
it was laid waste during the ravages of the Northmen.
When William the Red visited the site in 1092, it
is said to have been "desert" for more than two
hundred years.[a] William "restored the town, and
raised the castle; and drove out Dolphin, who before
had ruled the land there, and garrisoned the castle
with his own men. . . . . . And very many country
folk with wives and with cattle he sent thither, there
to dwell and to till the land."[b] A certain Walter, a
wealthy Norman priest, who had followed the Conqueror to England, was made governor of the new
town and castle. He began to build a church in

---

[a] "A Danis paganis ante cc. annos diruta, et usque ad id
empus mansit deserta."—*Flor. Wigorn.*

[b] Saxon Chronicle, ad ann. 1092.

honour of the Blessed Virgin, intending to found a college of secular canons in connexion with it. This was prevented by his death. But the church was completed by Henry I.; at the instance, it is said, of Adelulf, the second Prior of Nostel in Yorkshire, a house of Augustinian canons which had been established in 1121.[c] In 1133 the see of Carlisle was founded. Adelulf became the first bishop; the church of St. Mary became the cathedral; and, instead of secular, Augustinian canons were placed in the monastic buildings.[d] Carlisle was the only cathedral in England (and therefore in Christendom[e]) the episcopal chapter of which consisted of Augustinians.

II. Ancient authority for the architectural history of Carlisle Cathedral is so scanty that it can hardly be said to exist at all. From an indulgence recorded in the register of John le Romeyn, Archbishop of York, and dated in 1286, we learn that the church had some time before been "destroyed" by fire.[f] This "destruction" can only have embraced the choir,

[c] Godwin (de Episc. Carleol.), who cites no authority, and who confounds Adelulf, the second Prior of Nostel, with Ralf Adlave, the first Prior, and the founder of the house.

[d] The Augustinians may possibly have been established at Carlisle by Adelulf before the foundation of the see; but this is uncertain.

[e] The houses attached to all other monastic cathedrals in England were Benedictine. If there was ever an instance on the Continent (and this is doubtful) of a monastery attached to a cathedral, it also was Benedictine.

[f] This entry in the register (dated April 23, 1286) is mentioned by Raine, 'Lives of the Archbishops of York,' vol. i. p. 335.

which was a second time, and more completely, ruined by fire in 1292. An indulgence in consequence was issued by Archbishop Melton in 1318. In 1342 the revenues of Sowerby and Addingham were allotted by Bishop Kirkby as a fabric fund. The register of Bishop Welton (1353—1362) records that the building of the choir was in progress, and that collectors of alms for the fabric went as usual throughout the diocese. The register of Bishop Appleby (1363—1395) records the completion of the choir. The north transept had been greatly injured by the fire of 1292, and was afterwards rebuilt. It suffered again by fire in 1392, and was then restored by Bishop Strickland (1400—1419), who also rebuilt the central tower above the roof.

With the assistance of these dates, and from a careful examination of the building itself, it may be concluded that early in the thirteenth century the Norman choir (probably much smaller than that which now exists, see § IV.) was taken down, and that the building of a new choir, on the plan and foundations of the present, was commenced. It is not possible to determine with certainty at what time, or by whom, this Early English choir was begun. Mr. Ayliffe Poole suggests that Bishop Hugh (1219—1223) was the founder. Mr. C. H. Purday assigns the beginning, and perhaps the design, of the new building to Bishop Silvester of Everdon (1247—1254).[s] How-

---

[s] Mr. Purday's conclusions as to the dates of the several portions of the cathedral are to be found in an excellent 'Lecture

ever this may be, it is certain that the fires—before
1286 and in 1292—greatly injured, or in the usual
monastic phrase "destroyed" the choir. The aisle
walls, and some other portions, escaped on both occa-
sions; and the main arcade received its present form
after 1292.[h] The work then remained for some time at
a standstill; and it was not until the latter half of the
fourteenth century that the triforium and clerestory,
the eastern wall and the roof, were added, so as to
complete the choir.

Only a portion of the Norman nave remains, and
this, now serving as a parish church, is carefully
walled off from the cathedral.[i] A tradition, supported
by little or no authority, asserts that the greater part
of the nave was destroyed by the Scottish general,
Leslie, during and after the long siege of Carlisle in
1644-45.[k] The church, at any rate, seems to have

on the Architecture of Carlisle Cathedral,' Carlisle, 1859. Mr.
Purday was superintendent of the works during the restoration,
and had the best opportunities for making himself thoroughly
acquainted with the building. The judgment of the Rev. G.
Ayliffe Poole, as to the foundation of the choir, is so interesting
and important that it is given at length in an Appendix to
Part. I.

[h] See post, § VII.

[i] It is greatly to be wished that this part of the ancient
building should be restored to the cathedral. It was walled off
after the civil war, when the naves of some other English
cathedrals suffered the same fate, and were converted into parish
churches. The biographer of Seth Ward, Bishop of Exeter after
the restoration, records his removal of the "mighty Babylonish
wall" which had divided that cathedral into two parts.

[k] It is said that the materials were used to construct guard-

suffered from fire about this time; since Fuller, whose
'Worthies of England' was published in 1662, there
says that the cathedral "may pass for the embleme
of the Militant Church, black but comely, still bearing
in the complexion thereof the remaining signes of its
former burning."[1] Prince Charles Edward, during
his stay at Carlisle in 1745, nominated a certain James
Cappoch to the see, and installed him in the cathedral. (See Part II., *Bishop Fleming.*) The Jacobite
garrison of Carlisle were disarmed and confined in the
cathedral under guard. Much mischief, it is probable,
was then done in the church. "A beam lately taken
down from the nave-roof was covered with shot half
imbedded in its surface."[m]

Extensive restorations and repairs of the church
were commenced in 1853, and completed in 1857,

houses in the town, and that "this fact was proved during the
demolition of the fish market in 1858, by the discovery of many
fragments of moulded work, &c., brought from the cathedral."—
C. H. Purday. But at what time these fragments were so
brought does not appear. The cathedral walls near the ground
were (before the restorations) much disfigured by musket balls
and shot; and many of the mouldings showed, on close examination, that the soldiery had amused themselves with firing at
them.

[1] Worthies, Cumberland. Fuller is somewhat more laudatory
than certain 'officers' who visited many of the English cathedrals in 1634. "The next day wee repâyr'd to ther Cathedrall,
wch is nothing so fayre and stately as those we had seene, but
more like a great wilde country church; and as it appear'd out-
wardly, so was it inwardly, ne'er beautified nor adorn'd one
whit." '   [m] C. H. Purday.

under the direction of Mr. Ewan Christian, architect of the Ecclesiastical Commissioners. The cost was 15,000*l.* The cathedral is built throughout of sandstone from the neighbourhood; white or grey in the Norman portions, red in the choir.

III. In accordance with its history, so far as it has been ascertained, the existing cathedral displays portions of various dates.

Norman (1092—1130 ?)—South transept. Piers of central tower. Portion of the nave, now St. Mary's Church.

Early English (1219—1260 ?)—Walls and windows of choir aisles. St. Catherine's Chapel. Portions of main arcade ?

Early Decorated (*Geometrical*, 1292)—Portions of the main arcade of choir (the capitals were carved later).

Late Decorated (*Curvilinear*, 1353—1395)—Upper part of choir. East end and roof.

Perpendicular (1400—1419)—Upper part of tower.

Every part of the cathedral is interesting; but the flamboyant, or late Decorated work, is the especial distinction of Carlisle; and the east window, which is of this period, is perhaps the most beautiful in the world.

The cathedral is commanded by the castle, but is itself on high ground. The absence of a nave is of course the first point which strikes the visitor; but the beauty and grace of the remaining portion, crowned by its central tower, and surrounded by the picturesque

remains of the monastic buildings, soon draws attention to itself.   Trees and green sward, on the south
side especially, add not a little to the effect, con-
trasting as they do with the dark red stone of the
cathedral.   There is a good view of the cathedral
from the castle, whence it is seen to rise well over the
town, with the border hills beyond it.   An excellent,
and, indeed, the best, general view of both castle and
cathedral is that from the churchyard of Stanwix, a
suburb on the north bank of the Eden.   This churchyard marks the site of a small Roman outwork; and
it was by the road here descending the hill that
Scottish soldiers and forayers, the "host" led by the
Black Douglas and the Highlanders of 1745, approached the walls of "merry Carlisle."   From Stanwix the city is seen beyond the river, backed by the
distant outline of the Cumberland mountains.   Carlisle has become a manufacturing town, and the cathedral itself suffers from the close proximity of tall
chimneys, and the incessant stir and tumult of a great
railway station.   But the ancient associations of the
place cannot be destroyed.   Castle and cathedral alike
bear witness to days when, if the sun shone fairer on
Carlisle wall than at present, bishop and castellan
were seldom allowed to forget their position on the
limit of the English march.

IV. The cathedral is entered through the *south
transept*. The portal, richly and elaborately sculptured,
is entirely modern; and, however in keeping with the
late work of the choir, it has nothing in common with

the Norman portion of the church. The window above it is also modern.

The *transept*, here entered, is very shallow, projecting only one bay beyond the choir aisles. Dark, lofty, and narrow, its effect is altogether unusual. On the *east* side, a Norman arch with zigzag above it, and piers having plain cushioned capitals, opens to the choir aisle. South of this, a plain and massive Norman arch, of two orders, opens to St. Catherine's Chapel (see § VI.). The lower part of this arch is closed by late Decorated screen-work of great beauty, and deserving special attention (§ VI.). The chapel, as it now exists, is of later date; but each transept had originally a square Norman chapel projecting from it, and opening beyond a single arch. A similar arrangement, but on a larger scale, is traceable in the Norman transepts of Worcester Cathedral, but is not very usual. In the wall between the aisle and the chapel is a pointed doorway, formerly opening on a well which was closed during the late restorations. The water was raised by a windlass, and the arch was protected by a door with a massive bar. A similar well, regularly formed, and with sides of squared stone, exists in the north transept, but has long been covered. Besides supplying water for the use of the church, such wells may have been of especial service in border churches, which, like this of Carlisle, served as places of refuge for the inhabitants in case of sudden alarm or foray.ª (See *post*, Plate I.).

ª In the nave of Marden Church, Herefordshire, is a spring

The triforium above St. Catherine's Chapel has a plain, round-headed opening. The inner plane of the clerestory is of three arches, resting on shafts with carved capitals. The back of the central arch alone is pierced by a round-headed window.

On the *south* side, all except the actual wall is modern. The *west* side shows an arch, now closed, but once opening to the nave aisle. It is of the same general character as that opposite, as are the triforium and clerestory above it. The whole of this west wall is greatly out of the perpendicular, owing to the displacement of the piers of the Norman tower. The tower, no doubt, like most towers of the Norman period, had sunk and become insecure before the fire of 1392 (see § II.); after which it was rebuilt by Bishop Strickland (1400—1419). Strickland retained the Norman piers; but those which rise above them, of about equal height, with foliaged capitals, are, like the vaulting which they support, Perpendicular. On the capitals of the eastern arch are carved the badges of the Percy family—the crescent and fetterlock— perhaps to commemorate contributions for its erection

protected by stonework, and called St. Ethelbert's well. It is said to arise from the spot in which the body of St. Ethelbert was first interred. There is a well in St. Patrick's Cathedral, Dublin. In the choir of the church of St. Eloi, at Rouen, is a well, which gave rise to a proverb still in use there: "It is cold as the chain of the well of St. Eloi." The south transept of Ratisbon Cathedral contains a well, the stonework protecting which is sculptured with figures of Our Saviour and the woman of Samaria. See 'Notes and Queries,' 3rd series, vol. xii.

made by the famous Hotspur, who was at this time Governor of Carlisle and Warden of the Marches. On the west side of the tower are the rose and escallop shell—badges probably of the Dacres and Nevilles.

In the *north transept*, the Norman arch, once opening to the nave aisle, remains. There is an Early English window in the west wall, but the rest is entirely modern, and of Decorated character. Before noticing it, it will be better to pass from the cathedral into St. Mary's Church, where the remains of the *nave* may be examined, so far as high pews and galleries will permit. Only two bays exist, the piers of which are circular and very large, carrying plain round arches. The capitals on the north side are plain; those on the south have a leaf ornament. Semicircular wall-shafts run up to the bottom of the triforium, which has in each bay a wide, open, plain arch, pierced in the outer wall for light. The clerestory resembles that of the south transept. The arches nearest the tower are crushed out of place, and the aisle wall is much out of the perpendicular. Both nave and transept are said to have been covered with high pitched timber roofs.[o]

The whole of this Norman work is very plain and massive, agreeing well with the period (between 1092 and about 1130) at which it was erected. The Norman church was, as we know, complete before the creation of the see in 1133. The nave consisted of eight bays,

[o] In this church of St. Mary, Sir Walter Scott was married to Margaret Charlotte Carpenter, December 24, 1797.

and must have been grand and striking from its severe simplicity. The type is not that of Durham, which was in building at the same time, although the enormous piers of both cathedrals have something in common; nor can it be said to be that of the eastern cathedrals. The great circular piers of Malvern and of Pershore more resemble those of Carlisle, but are loftier. The Norman choir was of smaller extent than that which now exists, and probably terminated eastward in an apse.[p]

V. Returning to the transept, the later additions and alterations have to be noticed. The *north* transept

---

[p] This is the judgment of Mr. C. H. Purday, superintendent of the works during the restoration of the Cathedral. He adds, "Most writers upon this subject are, however, of a different opinion, and Mr. Billings . . . referring to a round-headed archway at the east end of the present choir, now blocked up, says, 'From this it is certain that the present east end was the extent of the Norman cathedral.' The archway in question, however, exhibits no trace of Norman workmanship, but, on the contrary, is clearly of later date. The round arch, in this case, forms no criterion of its date, as, although one of the great characteristic features of the Norman style, it was occasionally used long after the pointed arch had been universally adopted. Indeed, we have other examples of its employment in the choir. Mr. Billings also states that the south aisle of the choir was wider than the present one; but our restorations have disclosed a portion of the Norman wall in the angle near St. Catherine's Chapel, which proves that it was of the same width. The length of the original choir, according to my plan, would be 80 feet, the tower 35 feet square, and the nave 141 feet long; giving a total of 256 feet as the internal length of the Norman cathedral."—*Lecture on the Architecture of Carlisle Cathedral,* Carlisle, 1859.

was, as has already been said, rebuilt by Bishop Strickland at the beginning of the fifteenth century; but its north end has been again rebuilt during the late restorations. The large window, of geometrical character, has been filled with stained glass, as a memorial of five children of Dr. Tait, the present Bishop of London. All five died of scarlet fever between March 6 and April 9, 1858, at which time Dr. Tait held the Deanery of Carlisle. In the west wall the Early English window (late in design and showing plate tracery) is filled with stained glass, as a memorial of the Reverend Walter Fletcher, Chancellor of Carlisle, who died in 1846. The end of the transept is railed off, and forms the Consistory Court. Outside the rails, adjoining the arch of the choir aisle, is an altar-tomb, with a slab of black marble, bearing the inscription — "The tomb of Simon Senhouse, Prior of Carlisle in the reign of Henry VII. The original inscription being lost, the present plate was substituted by the senior male branch of the Senhouse family, A.D. 1850."

The arch opening to the choir aisle is Decorated. The Norman arch of the Norman choir aisle is seen built up in the wall between the present aisle and the entrance to the choir. (See § VII.)

Among the monumental tablets in the *north* transept is one with a head in medallion for M. L. Watson, sculptor; died 1847. There is also one for Robert Anderson, " the Cumberland Bard," who died in 1833; and one for Sir George Fleming, Bishop of Carlisle (1735—1747). In the west wall, protected by glass, is a stone,

WELL AND ST. CATHERINE'S CHAPEL.
CARLISLE CATHEDRAL.

with Runic inscription, found in its present position during the restoration. The words are — "Tolfihn yraita thasi rynr a thisi stain." "Tolfihn wrote these runes on this stone." The runes are Norse, not Anglo-Saxon. The latter are scarce in England, but Norse runes are still scarcer.[q] The inscription is not sepulchral. There have been three or four Tolfihns or Dolphins connected with Carlisle and its neighbourhood, and a chief of that name was governor here when William II. restored the town. (See *ante*, § 1.) "Possible it is that Tolfihn of Carlisle, proud of his Norse descent, had cherished the memory of his ancestors and their mode of writing; and it may well be that, upon one of the stones lying ready for the building of the south transept of the cathedral, he may, with the sharp pick of one of the workmen, have inscribed this memorial of his name."[r] The date of the inscription may, however, be the tenth, eleventh, or twelfth century. "Yraita," it is suggested, may be a Cumbrianism for the Icelandic "ritadi" (wrote).

VI. The beautiful screen-work (Plate I.) in the lower part of the arch opening to *St. Catherine's Chapel* is said to have been added by Thomas Gondibour, who became Prior in 1484; but the designs are decidedly characteristic of the flowing rather than of the Perpendicular period. They are, at any rate, of extreme

[q] On the font at Bridekirk, in Cumberland, is an inscription in the Anglo-Saxon language, but written with Norse runes.

[r] On an inscription in Runic letters in Carlisle Cathedral, by Edward Charlton, Esq., M.D.—*Archæologia Æliana*, new series, vol. iii.

grace and beauty.' St. Catherine's Chapel is of late Early English, or Early Decorated character. There are some fine brackets of foliage in the soffite of the arch between the chapel and the choir aisle. The chapel itself is now used as the choristers' vestry. A staircase ascends from it to an upper room, in which are some tiles and fragments of sculpture (some of the Roman period), found during the restoration; but not the "cornu eburneum," laid on the altar by Henry I. when he endowed the cathedral—a venerable relic long preserved here, but which has altogether disappeared.

VII. Through a low portal in the woodwork of the stalls the *choir* is entered. This portal is in the north-west corner of the choir; and it will be seen that the eastern tower arch fills only a portion of the west end of the choir, a flat wall projecting awkwardly beyond it on the north side. This is owing to the enlargement of the choir after the first great fire, toward the middle of the thirteenth century. The space which had before been filled by the north choir aisle was then taken into the choir itself, and a new aisle was added, beyond the ancient foundations. This was probably owing to want of room on the south side, where the conventual buildings pressed on the church; but the result is to

---

• These and other portions of the woodwork in the cathedral are figured in 'Illustrations of Geometric tracery from the Panelling belonging to Carlisle Cathedral,' by R. W. Billings, fol., London, 1848. This work consists of twenty plates, each giving a single panel of screen work, and the mode of drawing it. Thirteen of these plates are from the Chapel of St. Catherine alone.

CARLISLE CATHEDRAL. THE CHOIR

disfigure very unpleasantly the view from the east end
of the choir.

The first impression on entering the choir (Plate II.)
is produced by its rich and unusual colouring. The
warm red of the sandstone—the roof blue, powdered with
golden stars—the great east window filled with stained
glass, and the dark oak of the stalls—make up a picture
that enforces attention before the architectural details
—the noble main arcade, or the graceful tracery of the
east window—can receive their due admiration. The
choir of Carlisle is, architecturally, in no respect inferior to the choir of any other English cathedral of the
Decorated period; and it may be questioned whether,
in the two features already mentioned, it is not entitled
to the first place.

The choir is of eight bays; the two extreme bays,
east and west, are narrower than the others, and the
mouldings of the easternmost arches die into the wall
on either side of the great window. The presbytery is
raised by two steps above the choir, and the easternmost bay, in which stands the altar, by three. The
piers of the main arcade are Early Decorated; and the
whole arcade was certainly brought into its present form
after the fire of 1292. The capitals of the piers, however,
must have been at first unworked, since their beautiful
sculpture is of the Curvilinear (late Decorated) period.
There can be no doubt as to the date of these piers and
capitals; but the arches which they carry offer some
difficulty, and their mouldings and dog-tooth ornament
can only be explained by supposing that the Early

English arches were underbuilt after the fire of 1292,[t] or that, in the rebuilding, an earlier style was adopted for this portion of the arcade. Bishop WELTON (1353 —1362) and Bishop APPLEBY (1363—1395) carried on the work with much zeal; and the upper part of the choir (triforium, clerestory, and roof), together with the east end, must be assigned to this period (1353—1395).

VIII. The main arcade of the choir deserves special attention. The piers are octagonal, with larger shafts at the cardinal points, and smaller between. These secondary shafts are ribbed. All are of red sandstone. The bases have a deep and very effective hollow moulding. The arches which these piers support are very graceful, sharply pointed, of thoroughly Early English character, and are much enriched with the dog-tooth; large in the inner moulding, smaller in the label or exterior. The masonry of the main piers and of the wall above, up to the base of the triforium, is more even and regular in its courses than that of the upper stages.

The capitals of the piers and the small heads at the intersections of the arches were probably sculptured after the work was recommenced by Bishop Welton.

---

[t] This is the judgment of Mr. Ayliffe Poole. "I do not hesitate to say that the choir arcades are Decorated up to and including the capitals, then that the arches are Early English, and the triforium and clerestory Decorated again, *i.e.*, I believe that an Early English arcade was *underbuilt* with piers, and *overbuilt* with triforium, &c., of the next style—the Early English being Hugh of Beaulieu's—the rest the results of the fire in 1292."—*G. A. P.*

The foliage of the capitals, very sharp and effective, is certainly of flowing character, although here and there it retains the more decided naturalism of the earlier period. Mingled with the foliage are various small figures of men, animals, and monsters, all curious and interesting. Some of these represent the seasons. On the easternmost pier of the south side is a three-faced giant, eating at once with two of his mouths; and on the adjoining pier a winged creature, whose tail ends in a serpent's head, which twists round and bites the human head of the monster. The small heads at the intersections are good and characteristic. Marking the division between choir and presbytery is, south, a projecting dog-headed figure, and, north, the head of a queen.

The *triforium* has three arches in each bay (except the eastern and westernmost, which have only two), filled with Curvilinear tracery. The *clerestory* has a double plane; the inner of three lofty arches (that in the centre being the highest), with a parapet in front, pierced with quatrefoils. In the exterior plane are three fine windows, filled with Curvilinear tracery. Brackets of foliage, springing from the base of the triforium, support triple vaulting shafts, ringed at the base of the clerestory parapet, and having foliaged capitals. The sculpture is fine, but is far more conventional than that of the piers.

The remarkable ceiling of the choir was concealed in 1764 by a vaulting of plaster. This has happily

been removed, and the wooden ceiling, thoroughly and
well restored, has been painted under the direction of
Mr. Owen Jones.   The original colouring was red and
green; and it is somewhat to be regretted that the
restoration was not as strictly conservative here as in
the woodwork itself.   The ceiling is " semicircular in
form, boarded, and divided into square panels by
moulded ribs, with carved bosses at the intersections.
From the feet of three of the main ribs project what
are usually called hammer beams, terminated by large
angels, and connected with the vaulting shafts by wall
pieces and curved ribs.   As far as I am aware, there is
no other ancient example existing where the hammer
beams are introduced in a similar manner, and it seems
difficult to conjecture the purpose they were intended
to serve.   Mr. Billings suggests that lamps were suspended from them." [u]   This is possible; but the good
effect of these projections is at least doubtful, and so
far as they are concerned, it is hardly to be desired
that the ceiling of Carlisle should serve as an example.

IX. The east end of the choir is almost entirely
filled by the window.   (See Plate II. and the Frontispiece).   Of this, the jambs, with their slender
shafts and capitals of foliage, may perhaps be of
earlier date than the tracery, and possibly belong to the
same period as the main arcade of the choir.   The tracery
should probably be assigned to the episcopate of Bishop
Appleby (1363—1395).   The stone-work of all this

[u] C. H. Purday.

part is entirely new, although it reproduces most minutely the original design.

This famous window has in its lower part more lights or divisions (they are nine in number) than any other Decorated window in existence. Its upper portion exhibits (we may here adopt without reserve the judgment of Mr. Fergusson) "the most beautiful design for window tracery in the world. All the parts are in such just harmony the one to the other—the whole is so constructively appropriate, and at the same time so artistically elegant—that it stands quite alone, even among the windows of its own age."[x] The south window of the great transept in Lincoln Cathedral (*circ.* 1350) is nearly of the same date and character; but, "though extremely beautiful, it wants the perfect subordination which is so satisfactory in the example at Carlisle."[y] The west window of York, inserted by Archbishop Melton (1317—1340), has generally been regarded as a more serious rival of the Carlisle window. It is not so large, and, according to some critics, it is more completely "one vast design, of which no part is perfect without the rest."[z] It is no doubt earlier in date than the east window of Carlisle. (See York Cathedral, Pt. I. § xi.) The west window of Durham (see that Cathedral, Pt. I. § xii.) was the work of Prior Forcer (1341—1374), and was partly copied from that of York.

[x] 'History of Architecture.' The tracery of this window is said to be composed of 86 pieces, struck from 263 centres.

[y] Fergusson, *id.*

[z] Poole and Hugall, York Cathedral, p. 68.

It is, however, by no means so fine; and if Carlisle
must be placed highest, York is unquestionably entitled
to a position of but slight inferiority.

The stained glass which fills the tracery of this window is ancient, dating from the reign of Richard II.,
and represents the Resurrection, the Last Judgment,
and the New Jerusalem. The glass in the lower lights
is by HARDMAN, and was placed in the window in 1861
as a memorial of Bishop Percy, who died in 1856.
The subjects are from the Life of our Lord, having the
Crucifixion in the centre. The modern glass, although
good, contrasts not too agreeably with the ancient; but
its blue colouring assists in subduing the brilliance of
the gorgeous ceiling, which, without such a foil, would
be somewhat oppressive.

X. The view, looking west, is spoilt by the awkward
projecting wall on the north side of the tower arch (see
ante, § VII.). The organ, by Willis, and elaborately
diapered by Hardman, fills the arch itself from side to
side.

The *stalls*, with their canopies, which occupy the
three westernmost bays of the choir, are tolerably good,
but are by no means equal to the very fine wood-work
at Chester or at Manchester. Like the stalls in those
cathedrals, they are of late Perpendicular date, and
are said to have been erected by Bishop STRICKLAND
(1400—1419). The elbows of the stalls at the north-
west and south-west angles are carved with the head of
a king, apparently representing Henry IV. The subsellia are indifferently sculptured, chiefly showing gro-

tesques and fighting monsters. The tabernacle-work above is assigned to Prior Haithwaite, after the year 1433.[a]

The westernmost bay of the presbytery, on the north side, is closed by a fine screen, erected, between 1542 and 1547, by Lancelot Salkeld, the last Prior and first Dean. "Here the Gothic element is scarcely perceptible, most of the carving being a revival of classic forms and ideas."[b] In the upper panels are the initials L. S. (Lancelot Salkeld) and D. C. (Decanus Carleolensis). The rest of the woodwork in the choir, including the bishop's throne and the pulpit, dates from about the middle of the last century.

On the floor of the choir is the large brass of Bishop BELL (1478—1495). The figure is fully vested, and, what is unusual before the Reformation, holds a book.

XI. Through Prior Salkeld's screen we pass into the *north choir aisle.* Here the fine bases of the main piers are well seen, and from this side also the sculpture of the capitals should be examined. A broad stone plinth with panelled front extends between the bays, and on it the stalls rest.

The north wall of the aisle is of late Early English character (*circ.* 1230). The windows, of two lights, with their slender shafts, deep mouldings, and hollows filled with small dog-tooth, are very good. (They should be compared with the windows, also Early English, but later, in the western bays of the south aisle. It will be seen that a considerable advance in

[a] C. H. Purday.   [b] Id.

the style was made when the thick wall between the lights was replaced by a light mullion.) Triple vaulting shafts rise between each bay ; and the outer arch moulding of the windows is continued in each bay, and on either side, down to the top of the capitals of the vaulting shafts. In each window the capitals of the central shafts are enriched with leafage; the others are plain.

In both aisles, the third bay from the east (including the bay of the retrochoir), was altered by Prior Gondibour (1484), who replaced the Early English lights by a large Perpendicular window. These windows, with very doubtful judgment, since they were ancient insertions and marks in the history of the building, have been removed during the late restorations, and their place has been filled by Early English work, of the same design as the rest of the aisles.

Below the windows runs a very graceful wall arcade, of four foliated arches in each bay. The vaulting of the aisle is plain quadripartite, and seems to have been constructed, probably with earlier materials, after the fire of 1292. This Early English character ends eastward in the last bay of the choir aisle. The extreme eastern bay belongs to the retrochoir; and in this, the lower arcade, the window above, and the east window, are late Decorated, as is indicated by the mouldings and the different character of the leafage. In the westernmost bay of the aisle is a Perpendicular window; under which is a tablet for Bishop Law (1769—1787). The profile medallion is by J. Banks, R.A. The half-arch in the wall is the old buttressing arch of the tower. The pillar inserted in the north wall here is of the same date as the aisle, and apparently indicates that there was an intention to rebuild the transept, for which this was a preparation. "Some have supposed that a chapel was erected here, and has since been destroyed; but this could not have been the case, as the Norman east wall of the transept was not removed, but only cut away sufficiently for the erection of the pillar inside."[c] Opposite is a very fine bracket of foliage.

In the second Early English bay, from the east, are two very remarkable sepulchral recesses (Title-page) of the same date as the rest of the aisle, and no doubt intended, as Mr. Purday has conjectured, "to receive the effigies of the founders of this portion of the edifice." The nearly flat arch of each recess is enriched with a sort of chevron moulding, which, as it would seem, has not been found elsewhere. The points of each chevron are so much broken that the true character of the ornament has seldom been detected, and it has passed for an imitation of a stock or branch of a tree. One or two, however, remain perfect, so as to show the original design; and the engraving on the Title-page represents the recesses with the mouldings (which must have been very striking and effective), in their unbroken condition. In the easternmost recess is the effigy of a bishop, of Early English date, whose pectoral cross and mitre have been jewelled. It is perhaps the effigy of SIL-VESTER OF EVERDON (1247—1254), during whose epis-

[c] C. H. Purday.

copate, as has been conjectured by Mr. Purday (see
ante, § II.), the rebuilding of the Norman choir may
have been commenced. But the other recess is unap-
propriated; and Mr. Poole, with much probability,
sees in this fact an additional reason for assigning the
commencement of the Early English choir to Bishop
Hugh of Beaulieu, for whom this tomb may have been
prepared. He died at La Ferté, in Burgundy, and
was there buried. (See Appendix to Part I.)

In the bay east of these recesses is a large aumbrie,
and the very curious small mural brass of Bishop
ROBINSON (1598—1616). Robinson was for many years
Provost of Queen's College, Oxford; and a brass, which
is nearly a fac-simile of this at Carlisle, remains in the
chapel of Queen's. The bishop wears a linen rochet,
a black (?) chimere open in front, with lawn sleeves
attached to it, and a scarf. He has a skull cap, and in
his hand a pastoral staff, having inscribed on the shaft
" Ps. 23. Corrigendo, sustentando." On the crook,
" Vigilando, dirigendo." These words encircle an eye.
On a short veil or vexillum, suspended from the crook,
is the word " velando." Behind the kneeling figure of
the bishop appear the cathedral and the school, below
which are the words " Invenit destructum, reliquit
extructum et instructum." Three sheep-folds, over
which the bishop is watching, are represented in the
brass, which, like many of this late period, must
have been the work of some engraver of copper-plates
for books.

The back of the stalls in this aisle is painted with

designs from the life of St. Anthony, the hermit; and others from that of St. Cuthbert, very much injured. The central panels have figures of the twelve Apostles, each with a sentence from the Creed above him. On this painting are the initials of Thomas Gondibour, who became Prior of Carlisle in 1484. Richard Bell, who was at this time Bishop of Carlisle, had been Prior of Durham; and it was probably under his auspices that the deeds of the great saint of "the bishopric" were recorded in this place. The dresses and details, all of the end of the fifteenth century, deserve notice.

An inscription on the floor of the aisle marks the tomb of Archdeacon Paley and of his two wives. The 'Horæ Paulinæ' and the 'Evidences of Christianity' were written by him at Carlisle. A plain tablet for Paley is inserted in the wall below the east window of the aisle, where is also a piscina, marking the site of an altar.

XII. The narrow *retrochoir* or *procession-path* is now confined to the easternmost bay of the choir, at the back of the altar. This bay, as has already been said, is much narrower than the rest; and it seems most probable that the high altar, before the changes of the sixteenth century, stood one bay farther westward than it does at present.

The *south-choir aisle* is of the same general date and character as the north, with the exception of the windows in the two westernmost bays, which are still Early English, but of more developed character (see *ante*, § XI.). The easternmost bay (or that of the

P

retrochoir) is Decorated. The capitals of the Early English shafts in this aisle are less enriched than those opposite.

The view looking across the choir from either aisle is especially striking; and the very fine bases of the main arcade, the rich capitals, and the warm colouring of the stone, combine to render the aisles themselves very impressive. In the south aisle there is a plain sepulchral recess in the third bay from the east, and in the westernmost bay is the effigy of a bishop, usually assigned to Bishop BARROW (1423—1429). It is, however, certainly of an earlier period; and Mr. Purday is perhaps right in assigning it to Bishop WELTON (died 1362), under whom' (see *ante*, § VII.) the choir was nearly completed. The effigy is fully vested, but the head of the pastoral staff has disappeared. "The disposition and execution of the drapery are especially graceful and artistic."[d]

Against the wall of the choir is a tablet for Dean Cramer, died 1848: "Apud Oxonienses Historiæ Professor Regius."

The very beautiful Early English brackets in the soffite of the arch opening from the aisle to St. Catherine's Chapel deserve attention. The screen here was, like that in the transept (§ VI.), the work of Prior Gondibour; and, like that, is distinguished by its minute carving and graceful design.

The painting at the back of the stalls, also the work of Prior Gondibour, remains only in one bay. It

[d] C. H. Purday.

CARLISLE CATHEDRAL. SOUTH VIEW.

represents scenes from the life of St. Augustine, the
patron of the canons attached to the cathedral. The
verses which describe each subject are curious, and
worth reading. In one of the compartments the devil
appears to St. Augustine, bearing an enormous book.
From his mouth issue the words, "Pœnitet me tibi
ostendisse libros." * As in the north aisle, all the
details represented are of the end of the fifteenth
century.

XIII. Through the portal of the south transept we
again pass to the *exterior* of the cathedral. (Plate IV.,
the details of the south side are here shown.) In the
choir aisles the two eastern bays on the south side, and
all those on the north (the narrow easternmost bay on
either side is late Decorated, and belongs to the retrochoir), of the first Early English period (see *ante*,
§ XI.), show "an arcade of four divisions, having
detached shafts, with moulded bases, bands, and capi-

* This is an illustration of the story which asserts that the
Devil one day appeared to St. Augustine, carrying a book. The
Saint asked what the book contained, and was answered, "The
sins of men." He then adjured the Devil to show him any
passage in which his own sins were recorded, and found that the
only entry against him was that on one occasion he had neg-
lected to repeat the office of Compline. Commanding the Devil
to await his return, Augustine entered a neighbouring church,
and repeated the office. The entry in the book at once disappeared, and the Devil greeted St. Augustine as he came out of
the church with the words, "Turpiter me decepisti. Penitet
me quod librum meum tibi ostendi; quia peccatum tuum ora-
tionum tuarum virtute delesti." And so he disappeared in confusion. See the Golden Legend of Jacques de Voraigne, fol.
clxi.

tals, and effectively moulded arches. The two central divisions, wider than the others, are pierced by lancet windows. The cornice and plain parapet are carried by moulded blocks, with the nail-head enrichment. The effect of the whole is rich and beautiful." [f] The buttresses are without offsets, and gurgoyles (on the south side) project from them, somewhat unusually, instead of from the cornice. In both aisles, the second Early English bay from the east is entirely new, replacing Prior Gondibour's window (see § XI.). In the south aisle, the windows of St. Catherine's Chapel, and those in the two next bays, show an advanced Early English (see § XI.), but are not so effective as those in the eastern bays. In the third bay (from the west) are indications of a doorway and of a passage above it, difficult of explanation, since the eastern walk of the cloisters ran in a line with the south transept. The exterior of the clerestory has in each bay a triple arch, of which that in the centre, highest and widest, is pierced for light. Like this window, the heads of the blind arches on either side are filled with flowing tracery.

The *east end* (Frontispiece), almost rebuilt as it has been, is very striking. Massive buttresses rise on either side of the beautiful window, which descends unusually low. In either buttress are two richly canopied niches (the lowest nearly on a level with the spring of the window arch), containing figures of St. Peter, St. Paul, St. James, and St. John. The buttresses terminate in

[f] C. H. Purday.

five pinnacles; and the gable which rises between, crowned by a floriated cross, has, on either side, four somewhat similar crosses springing from its crockets of foliage. A beautiful triangular window, with a niche below it, containing a small figure of the Blessed Virgin with the Divine Infant, pierces the wall of the gable. Buttresses with very rich pinnacles terminate the aisles on either side. A row of houses has been cleared away from this end of the cathedral, so as to allow an uninterrupted view of one of the most beautiful late Decorated compositions in England.

Little can be said for the *central tower*, the work of Bishop STRICKLAND (1400—1419). Although not unpicturesque, especially as seen from the north and north-east, it does not equal in dignity the tower of many a parish church. A small watch-turret rises at the north-east angle. In a niche on the north side is an angel bearing a shield.

XIV. The scanty remains of the Norman nave are on the exterior plain and simple, although the general design must have been very effective. The cornices are supported by grotesque heads, "which even in their present weather-worn condition retain a wonderful amount of life and expression. Look attentively at those on the south side when the morning sun shines on them, and you will be struck by their life-like appearance."[g] According to Mr. Purday, who has had the best possible opportunities for ascertaining the fact, the whole of this Norman exterior was stuccoed

[g] C. H. Purday.

over, the joints marked in red lines, and the mouldings picked out with various colours. "Remains sufficient to prove this fact have been uncovered in various
places during the restorations. It was this coat of
external plaster which, I think, has contributed in a
great degree to the preservation of Norman stone-
work."[h] The sandstone of the Norman cathedral is
white, darkened of course by time and exposure; but
it contrasts remarkably with the red stone of the
choir.

XV. The *conventual buildings* were arranged, as usual,
round a cloister on the south side of the nave. On
the *east* side, and in a line with the south transept, the
arch remains which once opened to the vestibule of
the chapter-house, and beyond it the plainer portal
of the chapter-house itself. On the *south* side the
refectory remains entire, and now serves for the choir
school and the chapter library. It is (except the vault
on which it is raised, which is Decorated) of the late
Perpendicular period, *circ.* 1490. The canopied niches
in the north wall, and the reader's pulpit, deserve
attention; and the whole exterior, grey and ivy-clad,
is picturesque. There is a good general view of the
cathedral, in which the building groups well with its
surrounding trees, near the east end of the refectory.
Some traces of the dormitory vault exist on the west
side of the cloister garth, but the building above has
disappeared.

The *deanery* beyond the refectory was the prior's

[h] C. H. Purday.

lodge, and was nearly rebuilt by Prior Senhouse, *circ.* 1507. It contains one very fine room of perhaps earlier date, the ceiling of which has shields of arms, various devices, and, on the beams, some quaint verses.

The *abbey gatehouse* at the north-west corner of the close was the work of Prior Slee, 1527. It is a plain, round-headed archway, with the inscription, "Orate p̄ anima Christofori Slee, Prioris, qui primus hoc opus fieri incipit, A.D. MDXXVII."

CARLISLE CATHEDRAL.

APPENDIX TO PART I.

THE following remarks by the Rev. G. Ayliffe Poole, on the probability that the Early English choir of Carlisle was begun by Bishop Hugh of Beaulieu, are extracted from 'A Synchronistical Table of English Bishops,' printed in the Report of the Associated Architectural Societies for 1852, pp. 15, 16. Since the paper was written, proof (see Pt. I., § II. and note) has been afforded that Carlisle Cathedral had been much injured by fire before the greater fire of 1292. But Mr. Poole's argument is not affected by this discovery :—

"All the histories of Carlisle Cathedral tell us that the priory church was converted in 1132 (? 1133) into a cathedral, and remained in the state in which it was erected till 1292, when the whole building eastward of the tower, together with the north transept, was destroyed by fire." (Since this was written, however, it has been proved that a fire had occurred before 1286.) "If this history were true, we should have a Norman nave and south transept, as indeed we have, with a geometrical choir, with perhaps some Normain remains still visible; at all events no trace of Early English work would be visible. But, in fact, we have a choir of great width, as compared with the nave, with fine Early English aisles, and with traces of Early English which cannot be misunderstood in the pier arches; and we have also proofs that there was an Early English north transept. I purposely omit after changes, though they are extremely interesting, and involve one of the most curious cases of restoration that I know : all I want now is to observe that we have an Early English choir, and that of a very high order, and quite out of proportion with the ancient nave, not only ignored in the history, but positively excluded by the assertion that the Norman church remained in the same state in which it was erected till 1292.

"Now, I look at my list and find that the see was vacant from 1186 to 1218—no less than thirty-two years" (this, however, see Pt. II., is doubtful; two bishops, William and Bernard, are recorded in the interval, but little is known of them, and it is quite uncertain whether they ever visited their diocese. They are accepted as Bishops of Carlisle, however, both by Godwin and by Stubbes ['Registrum Sacrum Anglicanum'])—"and that then one Hugh was made bishop. Bishop Hugh's appointment accords very well with the style of the Early English choir; it also accords with a natural presumption that the restoration of a bishop to a church so long widowed would be signalised by some changes in the fabric. But can I get still further? Was Hugh a likely man to move in the matter? Yes, none more likely; for we have this very significant fact, that he was Abbot of Beaulieu in Hampshire. Now Beaulieu was founded by King John in 1204, and the buildings, which were of great splendour, were still in progress when Hugh, the first or second abbot—for both were of that name—accepted the bishopric of Carlisle; for Beaulieu was not finished and consecrated till 1246. Abbot Hugh left, therefore, a splendid Early English church in progress, to come to a poor and most likely half-ruined Norman one. Did he not take advantage of the stimulus naturally given to ecclesiastical affairs in Carlisle by the restoration of the see, to build a church more like that which he had left? The history says he did not, i. e. by implication; but the history *must* be wrong in declaring that no changes were made till 1292; and I believe you will infer with me that Hugh of Beaulieu is the prelate who is deprived of his just claim on the thanks of the church of Carlisle.

"But we have not yet done with Bishop Hugh of Beaulieu.

. . . . We find that he died at La Ferté, in Burgundy. Now, in the north aisle of the choir of Carlisle, in the usual place of a founder's tomb, and clearly contemporary with the fabric, is an empty sepulchre. If we are right in assigning the choir in question to Hugh, the tomb is empty because Hugh, for whom it was prepared, died abroad. I cannot but think that this is more than a slight confirmation of our former inferences. Again, therefore, we conclude that the choir which history places after 1292 was really the work of Hugh Beaulieu soon after 1218."

CARLISLE CATHEDRAL.

PART II.

History of the See, with Short Notices of the principal Bishops.

THE city of Carlisle (civitas quæ vocatur Lugubalia[a]), with a circuit of fifteen miles, was granted to St. Cuthbert and his successors by King Egfrid of Northumbria, during a synod held at Twyford on the Alne in 685.[b] Carlisle remained under the jurisdiction of the Bishops of Lindisfarne Chester-le-Street and Durham until the death of Ralph Flambard in 1128. The see of Durham was afterwards vacant until 1133; and in the mean time Thurstan, Archbishop of York, persuaded Henry I. to erect Carlisle into an episcopal see, with Cumberland and Westmorland for its diocese. The wiles and the instability of Flambard had no doubt led in part to this dismemberment of his diocese; but Thurstan was well aware that hitherto there had been little ecclesiastical supervision throughout the ancient Cumbria, and having himself seen the church which the Norman Walter had commenced in Carlisle, and which Henry I. had completed (see Pt. I., § 1.), he knew that

[a] So it is named in the Charter of Egfrid.

[b] It was at this synod that Cuthbert was elected Bishop of Hexham—the see which he exchanged in the same year for Lindisfarn. See Durham Cathedral, Part II. Egfrid's Charter will be found appended to Simeon's Hist. de Dunelm. Eccles. in Twysden's X. Scriptores, p. 57.

a cathedral for the future bishop was already provided. Accordingly, in 1133 (Aug. 6), Thurstan, in York Cathedral, consecrated Galfrid Rufus to the see of Durham, and

[A.D. 1133—1156.] ADELULF to that of Carlisle. Adelulf had been Prior of Nostel, in Yorkshire, a house of Augustinian Canons founded early in the reign of Henry I.[c] It is said that he was removed from Nostel to Carlisle by Henry, before the establishment of the see; that he was made Prior of the Augustinians, who, instead of secular canons, were placed in the church and convent which Walter had begun, and which King Henry finished; and that it was partly at his instigation that Carlisle was raised to an episcopal see.

Carlisle, although an important position on the Scottish border, can boast of few distinguished bishops. It was overshadowed by the greatness of the neighbouring see of Durham. After the death of Adelulf, the succession of bishops becomes very uncertain. A certain William is named as Bishop of Carlisle in 1174 : and for some time the see was vacant (probably owing to its scanty endowment) until

[A.D. 1203.] BERNARD, who had been Archbishop of Ragusa, was appointed to it. The year of his death is unknown.

[A.D. 1219—1223.] HUGH, the next bishop, had been Abbot of Beaulieu. See the Appendix to Pt. I., for some remarks on the probability of his having been the founder of the new choir. He died at the abbey of La Ferté, in Burgundy.

[A.D. 1224, resigned 1246.] WALTER MAUCLERC. He was Treasurer of England, and in 1233 was called to account on a false charge (as it would seem) for certain debts and defalcations. He attempted to carry his complaint to Rome, but was stopped on the eve of embarkation by the King's messengers, whom Roger, Bishop of London, excommunicated in consequence. Wearied and harassed, Bishop Walter

---

[c] He must not be confounded with *Ralph Adlave*, the founder and first Prior of Nostel.

resigned his see and became a Dominican at Oxford, where he died and was buried.

[A.D. 1247—1254.] SILVESTER OF EVERDON, Chancellor of England at the time of his election, an office which he long retained. He is said to have for some time declined the bishopric, saying that he was unworthy of it; and Matthew Paris records a speech of Henry III., when the Bishops of England entreated the King to abstain from promoting foreigners and unworthy persons. "It is known to all," said Henry, "how I raised thee, Silvester, to the episcopate—thee, the least of all my clerks—preferring thee instead of many theologians and reverend persons." [d] Little more is known of Silvester, who is said to have been killed by a fall from horseback. He was buried at Carlisle.

[A.D. 1255—1256.] THOMAS VIPONT, of the family of the Viponts, Earls of Westmorland. The see was vacant for two years.

[A.D. 1258—1278.] ROBERT DE CHAUSE, Chaplain to the Queen Eleanor of Provence, and apparently a foreigner.

The see remained vacant until

[A.D. 1280—1292.] RALPH IRETON was appointed. He had been Prior of Gisborough, the great Augustinian Priory in Yorkshire.

[A.D. 1292—1324.] JOHN OF HALTON, Canon of Carlisle. He died at Rose Castle, and was buried in his own cathedral.

[A.D. 1325—1332.] JOHN OF ROSS, Canon of Hereford; was intruded by the Pope.

[A.D. 1332—1352.] JOHN KIRKBY. In 1345 the Scots, under Douglas, plundered and burnt great part of Carlisle. Bishop Kirkby, with Sir Thomas Lucy and Sir Robert Ogle, pursued them, compelled them to fight at great disadvantage, and gained an easy victory.

[d] " Et te, Silvester Carleolensis, qui diu lambens Cancellarium, Clericorum meorum clericulus extitisti, qualiter postpositis multis theologis et personis reverendis, te, inquam, in Episcopum sublimavi, omnibus satis notum est." M. Paris, p. 746.

[A.D. 1353—1362.] GILBERT OF WELTON, was intruded by the
Pope, in opposition to John of Horncastle, Prior of Carlisle,
whose election had been confirmed by Archbishop Thoresby,
and who had even obtained restitution of temporals from
the King.

[A.D. 1363—1395.] THOMAS APPLEBY, Prebendary of York and
of Southwell (preferments which he retained after he became
bishop) and Warden of the Marches. The registers of
Bishops Kirkby, Welton, and Appleby, record the building
of the cathedral choir, and its completion under Appleby.
(See Pt. I., § II.)

[A.D. 1396, translated to Chichester 1397.] ROBERT READE,
Bishop of Waterford and Lismore, was translated by Papal
bull, issued at the request of Richard II. The Canons had
elected William Strickland, who was set aside. Reade was
a Dominican. He died in 1415.

[A.D. 1397, deposed 1399.] THOMAS MERKES, a Benedictine
of Westminster, also intruded by the Pope. Bishop Merkes
was a faithful adherent of Richard II., and in the first Parliament of Henry IV. protested against the deposition of
Richard and the assumption of the crown by Henry of Lancaster. For this offence the Bishop, who before the fall of
Richard had made himself specially hated by the Lancas-
trians, was at first committed to the Tower, and afterwards
to the custody of the Abbot of Westminster. He was
speedily released; but joining in the conspiracy of the Earls
of Kent, Salisbury, and others against Henry $\left(\dfrac{1399}{1400}\right)$ was
deposed by the Pope, who, however, made him Bishop of
Samos "in partibus infidelium." His life was, no doubt,
spared on account of his episcopal character. As yet no
bishop had been condemned to death in any court, secular
or spiritual. His see of Samor brought him no revenue;
but in 1404 Bishop Merkes was instituted to the rectory of
Todenham, in Gloucestershire, where he died and was buried
in 1409.

[A.D. 1400—1419.] WILLIAM STRICKLAND, member of an ancient Cumberland family, now became Bishop of Carlisle. His former election had been set aside in favour of Bishop Reade. Strickland was the builder of the existing tower (Pt. I., §§ IV. XIII.), and restored the north transept (Pt. I., § V.). The tower at Rose Castle was also built by him.

[A.D. 1420—1423.] ROGER WHELPDALE, educated at Balliol, and afterwards Provost of Queen's, Oxford. He died in London, and was buried in St. Paul's.

[A.D. 1423—1429.] WILLIAM BARROW, translated from Bangor.

[A.D. 1430—1450.] MARMADUKE LUMLEY, Treasurer of England, 25th Henry VI.; Chancellor of Cambridge. He was translated from Carlisle to Lincoln, where he died in the same year (1450).

[A.D. 1450—1452.] NICHOLAS CLOSE, Archdeacon of Colchester and Chancellor of Cambridge, was translated to Lichfield 1452, and, like his predecessor at Carlisle, died in the year of his translation.

[A.D. 1452—1462.] WILLIAM PERCY, son of the Earl of Northumberland.

[A.D. 1462—1463.] JOHN KINGSCOTE, Archdeacon of Gloucester.

[A.D. 1464—1468.] RICHARD SCROOPE, Chancellor of Cambridge.

[A.D. 1468—1478.] EDWARD STORY; was translated to Chichester, where he died in 1503.

[A.D. 1478—1495.] RICHARD BELL, Prior of Durham. It was in his time that the remarkable paintings at the back of the stalls in the cathedral choir, illustrating the life of St. Cuthbert, were executed. (See Pt. I., § XI.).

[A.D. 1496, translated to Durham in 1502.] WILLIAM SENHOUSE. (See Durham Cathedral, Pt. II.)

[A.D. 1503—1508.] ROGER LAYBURN, President of Pembroke Hall, Cambridge.

[A.D. 1509—1520.] JOHN PENNY; was translated from Bangor.

[A.D. 1521—1537.] JOHN KITE had been consecrated Archbishop of Armagh by Papal provision in 1513; but afterwards resigned that see and became titular Bishop of Thebes. He was buried in Stepney church, near London.

[A.D. 1537—1557.] ROBERT ALDRICH, educated at Eton and at King's College, Cambridge; Provost of Eton, Canon of Windsor, and Registrar of the Order of the Garter. He was a friend and correspondent of Erasmus, who calls him "blandæ eloquentiæ juvenis."

[A.D. 1557, deposed 1559.] OWEN OGLETHORPE, Dean of Windsor, and President of Magdalene College, Oxford. He was made bishop by Queen Mary. "A good natured man," says Fuller, "and when single by himself very plyable to please Queen Elizabeth, whom he crowned Queen, which the rest of his order refused to do; but when in conjunction with other Popish bishops, such principles of stubborness were distilled into him that it cost him his deprivation. However, an author (Sir John Harrington) tells me that the Queen had still a favour for him, intending his restitution either to his own or a better bishoprick, upon the promise of his general conformity, had he not dyed suddenly of an apoplexie, 1559." [c] The see remained vacant for some months.

[A.D. 1561—1570.] JOHN BEST.

[A.D. 1570—1577.] RICHARD BARNES was consecrated at York suffragan Bishop of Nottingham in 1567. He was translated to Durham in 1577. (See Durham Cathedral, Pt. II.)

[A.D. 1577—1598.] JOHN MAY, Archdeacon of the East Riding, President of St. Catherine's Hall, Cambridge.

[A.D. 1598—1616.] HENRY ROBINSON, born in the city of Carlisle; Fellow and Provost of Queen's College, Oxford. "A prelate of great gravity and temperance; very mild in speech. . . . . When Queen Elizabeth received his homage she gave him many gracious words of the good opinion which she conceived of his learning, integrity, and sufficiency

[c] Worthies—Oxfordshire.

for that place; moreover adding 'that she must ever have a care to furnish that see with a worthy man, for his sake who first set the crown on her head'" (Bishop Oglethorpe).[f] The curious brass of Bishop Robinson remains in the north choir-aisle of his cathedral (Pt. I., § XI.).

[A.D. 1616—1621.] ROBERT SNOWDEN, Fellow of Christ's College, Cambridge; Prebendary of Southwell.

[A.D. 1621—1624.] RICHARD MILBOURNE, translated from St. David's. He had been Fellow of Trinity, Cambridge, and Dean of Rochester.

[A.D. 1624—1626.] RICHARD SENHOUSE, Fellow of St. John's, Cambridge, and Dean of Gloucester. Killed by a fall from horseback.

[A.D. 1626, translated to Norwich, 1629.] FRANCIS WHITE, Dean of Carlisle. From Norwich he was translated to Ely in 1631. Died 1638.

[A.D. 1629—1642.] BARNABAS POTTER, Provost of Queen's College, Oxford. "He was commonly called," says Fuller, "the puritanicall bishop; and they would say of him in the time of King James, that 'Organs would blow him out of the church;' which I do not believe; the rather because he was loving of and skilfull in Vocall Musick, and could bear his own part therein."[g]

[A.D. 1642—1656.] JAMES USSHER; the great and learned Archbishop of Armagh, was in England at the breaking out of the Irish rebellion in 1641; and the condition of Ireland prevented him from returning to his see. Charles I. gave him the vacant bishopric of Carlisle, to be held in commendam; although the revenues of Carlisle were at this time little more to be depended on than those of Armagh. Ussher never saw his northern diocese. The parliament gave him a pension of 400*l.* a year when the English bishops were deprived, and Cromwell treated Ussher with great courtesy and consideration. He died, March 21st.

[f] Fuller. Worthies—Cumberland, from Sir John Harington.
[g] Worthies—Westmorland.

Q

($16\frac{1}{3}\frac{5}{8}$) in the Countess of Peterborough's house at Reigate; and was buried by Cromwell's order in Westminster Abbey,

[A.D. 1660, translated to York, 1664.] RICHARD STERNE. See York Cathedral, Pt. II.

[A.D. 1664—1684.] EDWARD RAINBOW, Master of Magdalene College, Cambridge; Dean of Peterborough on the Restoration.

[A.D. 1684—1702.] THOMAS SMITH, Fellow of Queen's College, Oxford; Dean of Carlisle.

[A.D. 1702—1718.] WILLIAM NICHOLSON, Fellow of Queen's, Oxford; Prebendary and Archdeacon of Carlisle. He was translated to Derry in 1718; thence to Cashel in 1727; and died in the same year. Nicholson was an antiquary, and a man of considerable learning. His letters on the Runic inscriptions at Bewcastle and Bridekirk are inserted in Gibson's Camden. Bishop Nicholson is best remembered for his 'English Historical Library' (1696—1699), notes on the materials for English History, which at the time of their publication were of much value. He also compiled a Scottish and Irish 'Historical Library.'

[A.D. 1718—1723.] SAMUEL BRADFORD, Master of Christ's College, Cambridge; Prebendary of Westminster. In 1723 he was translated to Rochester, and died in 1731.

[A.D. 1723—1734.] JOHN WAUGH, Fellow of Queen's College, Oxford; Dean of Gloucester.

[A.D. 1735—1747.] SIR GEORGE FLEMING, Bart. Representative of the ancient family of Fleming of Rydal Park; Dean of Carlisle.

It was during the episcopate of Bishop Fleming that Charles Edward occupied Carlisle; and installed in the Cathedral, as bishop of the see, a Romanist named ꭲames Cappoch. Cappoch was afterwards hanged; having been found in the city at the time of its recapture by the Duke of Cumberland.

[A.D. 1747, translated to London 1762.] RICHARD OSBALDESTON. Died 1764.

[A.D. 1762—1768.] CHARLES LYTTELTON, brother of George, Lord Lyttelton; Dean of Exeter.

Bishop Lyttelton was President of the Society of Antiquaries. Many papers were contributed by him to the ' Archæologia.'

[A.D. 1769—1787.] EDMUND LAW.

[A.D. 1787—1791.] JOHN DOUGLAS, translated to Salisbury; died 1807. The friend of Goldsmith.

> " And Douglas is pudding, substantial and plain."
> *Retaliation.*

See Salisbury Cathedral, Pt. II., for a longer notice.

[A.D. 1791—1808.] EDWARD VENABLES VERNON HARCOURT translated to York; died 1847.

[A.D. 1808—1827.] SAMUEL GOODENOUGH.

[A.D. 1827—1856.] HUGH PERCY, was translated to Carlisle from Rochester.

[A.D. 1856—1860.] HENRY MONTAGUE VILLIERS, translated to Durham; died 1861.

[A.D. 1860.] SAMUEL WALDEGRAVE.

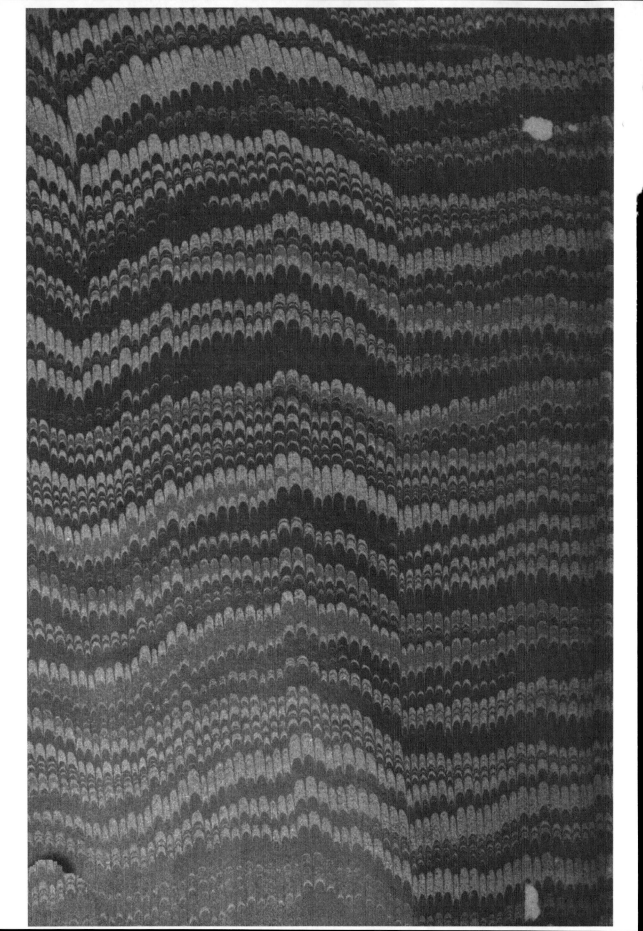

CPSIA information can be obtained at www.ICGtesting.com
Printed in the USA
LVOW02s2106010315

428826LV00016B/450/P